GREAT
CUSTOMER
SERVICE
ON THE
TELEPHONE

The WorkSmart Series

GREAT
CUSTOMER
SERVICE
ON THE
TELEPHONE

Kristin Anderson

amacom

AMERICAN MANAGEMENT ASSOCIATION
THE WORKSMART SERIES

New York • Atlanta • Boston • Chicago • Kansas City • San Francisco • Washington, D.C.
Brussels • Toronto • Mexico City

This book is available at a special
discount when ordered in bulk quantities.
For information, contact Special Sales Department,
AMACOM, a division of American Management Association,
135 West 50th Street, New York, NY 10020.

This publication is designed to provide accurate and authoritative information in regard to the subject matter covered. It is sold with the understanding that the publisher is not engaged in rendering legal, accounting, or other professional service. If legal advice or other expert assistance is required, the services of a competent professional person should be sought.

Library of Congress Cataloging-in-Publication Data
Anderson, Kristin.
  Great customer service on the telephone / Kristin Anderson.
    p.   cm.—(The WorkSmart series)
  ISBN 0-8144-7795-X
  1. Telephone in business.   2. Customer service.   I. Title.
II. Series.
HF5541.T4A45   1992
658.8'12—dc20   *92-22159*
                                                      CIP

Printing number

10   9   8   7   6   5   4   3   2   1

CONTENTS

PREFACE

Does anyone *not* know how to use the telephone? You probably can't even remember a time when speaking on the phone wasn't part of your everyday life. So why should you read this book?

Using the telephone *effectively* involves much more than simply picking up the handset, dialing seven or eleven numbers, and chatting with your favorite customer about your latest product breakthrough. Using the telephone *well* will benefit you both personally and professionally.

Whether you are a service professional spending seven hours a day (or more!) on the phone to customers, a manager or support person who uses the phone to talk to coworkers, or someone who makes only a few calls each week, the way you use the telephone will impact on how customers and coworkers feel about the quality of service your company provides. And positive customer feelings translate into increased profits, how your coworkers feel about their work environment, and how you feel about yourself and your job.

Bottom line: The way you use—or abuse—the telephone is critically important to you and your company.

Don't believe it? Consider the example below:

Receptionist: ErgibbitandAssociates. HowmayIhelpyou?

Joe [*hesitant*]: Is this *Flibb*ergibbit and Associates?

Receptionist [*snide*]: Yes. HowmayIhelpyou?

Joe: I saw your ad. I'd like to order a flibbergibbit.

Receptionist [*challenging*]: Do you have an account with us?

Joe: No, but—

Receptionist [*interrupting*]: Connecting you with new account services. (CLICK)

Joe [*to himself, while the phone rings*]: But I want to order it on my brother's account. (Still ringing) I don't *need* new account services. (Still ringing) And I don't need this! (CLICK)

Who lost in this transaction?

Joe lost. He didn't get to place his order, and he wasted his valuable time in the bargain.

Flibbergibbit lost. They lost Joe as a customer for this sale and probably for his repeat business. They may even have lost Joe's brother. And as Joe tells ten to fifteen people about his experience, at least five more people will decide Flibbergibbit is a company they never want to do business with.

Finally, Flibbergibbit's employees lost, too. They lost the sense of a job well done and the satisfaction of being able to connect their customer with just the right product or service.

In fact, *everyone* lost—company and customer alike.

DOUBLE YOUR EFFECTIVENESS ON THE LINE

In each chapter, *Great Customer Service on the Telephone* offers specific tips and techniques that will literally double your telephone effectiveness. You can read it straight through, cover to cover, or you can use the Table of Contents to zero in on a particular telephone talk challenge, be it taking a message or dealing with customer anger, and start there.

Keep this book near your phone and use it as a handy reference guide when you need a refresher on a particular telephone technique or help with handling a difficult call.

To help focus your effort, this book is divided into three parts: "Managing the Medium," "Managing Your Call," and "Managing Yourself." Short chapters within each part address specific telephone communication issues. At the end of the book are several informational appendix sections, including tips for placing international calls and charts of North American area codes and time zones.

This book focuses on using the telephone in a business setting. The person on the other end of the line is often referred to as the customer, but a customer can be anyone who looks to you for assistance. Any tip for phoning an *external* customer works equally well with your *internal* customers—your coworkers—and with your vendors—the service professionals who help you serve your customers.

But these tips and techniques will work for you even when you're not working—when you're using the telephone to communicate effectively with friends and family.

K.A.

ACKNOWLEDGMENTS

I'd like to extend my heartfelt thanks and appreciation to several of the people who helped make this book a reality: to Ron Zemke for giving me the time and encouragement; to Jill Applegate for assistance above and beyond the call of her job title; and to Beverly and Keith Anderson, my parents, who gave me my first lessons in service.

PART

MANAGING
THE MEDIUM

Dick Tracy can do it. So can George Jetson. But for the rest of us, combining visual images and telephone talk is still fiction. The telephone medium, by its very nature, limits and distorts communication. The physical apparatus of the telephone serves as a filter for everything you want to communicate to your caller and for everything your caller wants to communicate to you. When it isn't managed, that "filter" can—and will—work against you. It's no wonder that the real message can be so easily lost or garbled when you can't deliver it in person!

You *can* manage the telephone medium so that it is a powerful and positive tool that works for you. You manage it first by understanding it—what it does, and what it keeps you from doing. Then, you use the most effective techniques and tactics for taking messages, transferring calls, juggling lines, and taking advantage of the technology.

You probably won't use a Dick Tracy watch or a Jetson's View Phone, at least not in this decade. But you don't need one. By using the techniques given in this section, the power of communicating with far-off voices (the original Greek meaning of *telephone*) will be yours.

CHAPTER 1

YOU CAN BE A MIND READER

Whether your company makes cars, sells insurance, repairs air conditioners, or heals the sick; whether your customers are young or old, rich or poor, or men or women—you *can* know for certain what your customers expect. When it comes to calling your company on the phone, customers expect you to do two things:

1. Show respect.
2. Have a good reason for being on the other end of the line.

Showing respect means dealing with all calls in a pleasant and courteous way. You show through your voice and your manner that you are genuinely pleased to be having the conversation (even when the customer is complaining or saying "no" to your product offering!). Respect also means that you are not using the telephone as a weapon, a way to cheat or mislead the customer with "too good to be true" offers and services—which, of course, you would never do.

Having a good reason for being on the line means that there is a positive purpose in the call. If you're picking up the phone, it means that you *will* assist the caller in whatever way possible. You have a good reason even if all you can do at that moment is take a complete and accurate phone message and pass it on to the appropriate person. If you are placing the call, a good reason means that you are acting in good faith upon the belief that what you have to say will be beneficial to or of interest to the person you are calling.

GETTING INSIDE YOUR CUSTOMER'S HEAD

A funny thing happens when you pick up a ringing phone. To the caller, you *become* your company. It doesn't matter if you're the night janitor or the CEO. To the caller, *you are the company*.

During each call, you have an opportunity to create for your customer a positive memory of your organization—a memory of "the people with the friendly voices," or "the folks who have all the answers," or "the man who cared about my problem," or "the woman who helped me understand and get just what I needed."

To create positive memories, you must manage the five ways customers evaluate your telephone contact with them. These five keys, identified by Texas A&M researcher Dr. Leonard Berry and his colleagues, encapsulate everything your customer judges when he or she comes into contact with you:

1. *Reliability*. The ability to provide what was promised, dependably and accurately.
2. *Responsiveness*. The willingness to help customers promptly.
3. *Assurance*. The knowledge and courtesy you show to customers, and your ability to convey trust, competence, and confidence.

The next time you hang up after a call to a bank or a restaurant or a hairdresser or a doctor's office, pause a moment and ask yourself two questions:

1. **What memory did the voice on the other end of the line create for me?**
2. **Is this a memory I would want to create for my customers?**

---

4. *Empathy*. The degree of caring and individual attention you show your customers.

5. *Tangibles*. The physical facilities and equipment, and your own and others' appearance. (Think this one doesn't belong? Consider how poor telephone equipment *sounds* over the phone lines, and how often customers and coworkers see you when you're talking on the telephone.)

Use the worksheet below to list at least one way you demonstrate each factor when you use the telephone. For example, next to "Reliability" you might write "I return all phone messages within two hours or before 9:00 A.M. the following business morning."

HOW I MEET CUSTOMER EXPECTATIONS WITH MY TELEPHONE TALK

Reliability:

Responsiveness:

Assurance:

Empathy:

Tangibles:

Post the list of the Berry factors near your phone to remind yourself of ways you transmit positive memories through the telephone lines.

CHAPTER 2

THE CHALLENGE OF TELEPHONE COMMUNICATION

One of the most important aspects of your day-to-day interactions with customers and coworkers, friends and fam- ily, is your *nonverbal* communication—the things you *don't* say. The way you stand or move, the clothes you wear, the gestures you make, everything that you don't say sends a far stronger message than the actual words you use and even the way you use those words.

Given the subtlety and importance of nonverbal communi- cation, it's a wonder we can communicate over the telephone at all! And yet, for most businesses the telephone is a major lifeline—often the *number one medium* of communication. The telephone compresses time and space. It allows you to com- municate over long distances not possible with face-to-face communication. The telephone has an immediacy that the mail cannot rival. And it allows interaction in a way not possible through broadcast television or radio.

THE COMMUNICATION PROCESS

Whether you are communicating face-to-face or via the telephone, the communication process itself remains the same. Figure 1 illustrates the six elements involved in every communication act: (1) the sender, (2) the channel of com- munication, (3) the receiver, (4) feedback, (5) the physical environment, and (6) the sender and receiver's psychological environment.

Figure 1. The communication process.

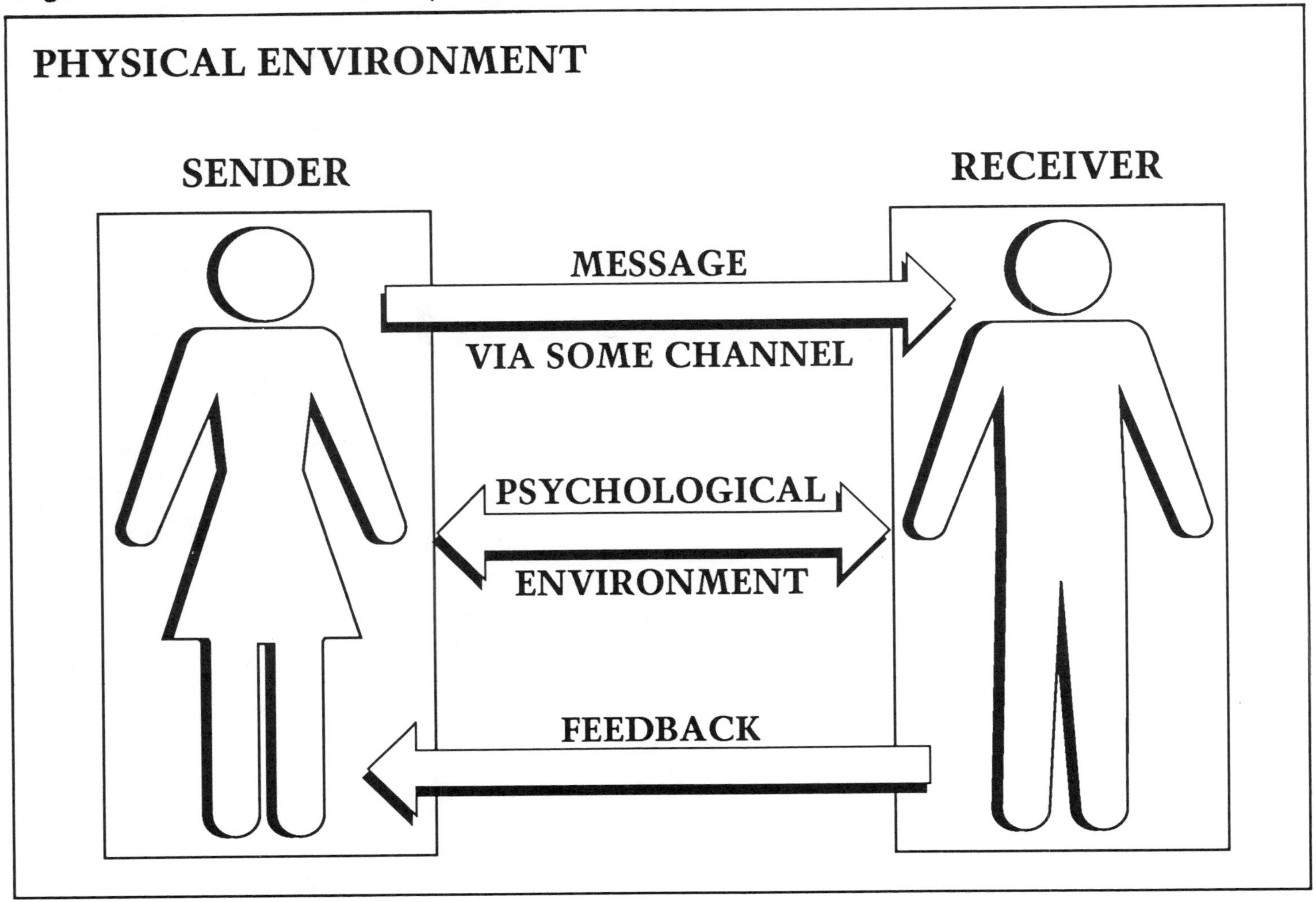

It is important to understand each of the six communication elements and how they interact:

Sender	The person with a message to communicate.
Channel of Communication, or Medium	The way the message will travel between sender and receiver.
Receiver	The person who hears the message and interprets its meaning.
Feedback	The way the receiver indicates that the message has been heard and understood—or that it is confusing or annoying. The receiver's response to the sender.
Physical Environment	What surrounds the entire communication process. It includes your work space and the physical place where your customer is and whether those places are warm or cold, noisy or quiet, and so on.
Psychological Environment	What both sender and receiver operate within, made up of their past experiences, fears and expectations, assumptions and prejudices. It affects how the sender shapes the message and how the receiver interprets it.

Whether you are sender or receiver during a phone conversation, you have 100 percent of the responsibility to make sure that the message is understood correctly. As sender, you must present your message in the way it will be best understood by the receiver. As receiver, you must provide feedback either by asking for clarification or acknowledging understanding.

When you communicate your message via the telephone, you have to craft it more carefully than when you communicate face-to-face. Effective phone communication is short and to the point, while remaining cordial. It includes requests for feedback as well as silent time to allow that feedback to be communicated.

The physical apparatus of the telephone can distort the sound of your voice and make your words difficult to understand. In addition, the telephone eliminates nonverbal communication, so the importance of verbal communication skills—including the way you manage subverbals such as "uh huh" and "hmmm" and other sounds you make to indicate you are listening—is increased.

One of the reasons that nonverbal communication is so powerful is that it gives us clues about a person's psychological environment. If you call a woman customer "Honey" in a face-to-face situation, and you see her eyes narrow and her face get red, it's a pretty clear indication that you've offended her. And after you see that, you have a chance to make things right. But when you talk on the telephone, when such clues are lacking, it is critically important that you know your caller's "hot buttons" *before* you place the call, or at least that you are extra sensitive to the way your message may be interpreted or misinterpreted by the person on the other end of the line.

Unlike face-to-face communication, telephone communication means that you and the caller will be in different physical environments. Your message may compete with distractions beyond your control—office noise, interruptions, uncomfortable temperature, or a large window overlooking a lake where your customer would rather be! Listen for background noise clues. They may prompt you to ask, "Is now a good time for our phone call?" or "Am I speaking loud enough?" When you compete with outside distractions, your telephone message has to be interesting to your caller and straight to the point.

CHAPTER 3

THERE'S A RINGING IN MY EARS!

You know what it feels like. You place a call and the telephone rings once, twice, three times, four times, six times, eight times. You wonder if you've dialed the wrong number or whether you've accidentally called Mars—and no one is home. Or, maybe the person you're calling is suffering an elbow malady that prevents him or her from picking up the phone. Or perhaps today is a new federal holiday and your company is the only one open for business.

Finally, you give up, abandon your attempt. You become yet another customer lost to an unanswered telephone.

It's precisely because of this all too frequent scenario that many companies have instituted a policy of "answer by the third ring." By setting a standard and measuring performance against it, companies hope they can eliminate a lot of customer frustration—and gain increased customer satisfaction.

Is there something magical about three rings? No. In fact, studies show that customers care *more* that their call is eventually answered by *someone who can assist them* than about the number of rings. At the same time, no caller has ever said, "Don't answer yet. I haven't waited long enough." So, three rings provides a convenient starting place when working to serve customers better via the telephone.

Whether or not your company has a standard for answering phone calls, you will want to have your own personal standard. It's a helpful way to track and improve your own performance—and to identify times when you need some assistance to make certain your telephone works for, and not against, you and your customers.

How fast *should* you answer the phone? Here are some things to consider:

- *Industry standards.* A customer's expectation of what is prompt may vary depending on whom he or she is calling. For example, a person may expect that a hotel's switchboard phone operator should answer on the second or third ring. That same person, however, may be prepared—and satisfied—to wait for five to eight rings when calling a government agency or a friend's home. What do customers in your industry expect? Three rings? Five rings *if* a human finally answers? You should meet or, better yet, exceed the standard answer time used in your industry. After all, your customer will compare you to your competition.

- *Consistency.* If your company sets a standard for answering customer phone calls, avoid the temptation of using a different standard when answering calls from other employees. If your phone system differentiates between *internal* and *external* calls, it's easy to think "that call can wait, it's just another employee." In reality, the way you answer calls from fellow employees—your internal customers—will affect the way you answer calls from external customers. If you are a manager, this is even more critical. Your behavior provides a model and sets the informal standard for the employees you supervise.

- *Voice messaging.* Many "three-ring" voice messaging systems are actually designed to take a phone call if it is not answered after 2½ rings. That's why when you try to pick up the call after the third ring, the caller isn't there—he or she is talking to your voice mail. If your company has such a system, make your personal standard to "answer on the first ring."

- *Rollover systems.* If your phone is part of a large system, you can probably set it to roll over to another line if the call is not answered by the third ring. This can be a terrific way to ensure that calls are answered. But be careful.

If you set your phone to roll over after three rings and the person at the rollover number isn't able to answer quickly, the customer may have to wait for six rings. Worse yet, the call may roll again to a third line. Some customers refer to this as being "trapped in the VOX from hell!"

ROLLOVER REMINDER

Have to leave your office for lunch? Need to step away to attend a meeting? Programming your telephone to "roll" to another number will ensure that your customers' calls are answered. The problem is remembering to reclaim your phone—to take it *off* of the rollover feature—when you return to your desk. Here are two tricks to help you remember:

1. If you have an older-model telephone, simply turn the handset upside down in the cradle.
2. Place a brightly colored "RECLAIM THE PHONE" note on your telephone, or, if your desk is cluttered, on your chair.

You'll find that a visual reminder works better than the realization, hours after you return to your desk, that "Gee, my phone hasn't rung in an awfully long time."

CHAPTER 4

TAKING MEANINGFUL MESSAGES

When you pick up a ringing telephone, you assume an important obligation—the obligation of communication. It doesn't matter whether your title is receptionist or CEO, fulfilling that obligation means taking a message. Perhaps it will be a message for yourself, so that you can return the call at a more convenient time or when you have more complete information. More likely, it will be a message for someone else. When that is the case, both the caller and the intended recipient depend on you to gather correct and complete information.

A good friend recently had a medical emergency that put him in intensive care. More than a bit "out of it," Tommy Polk couldn't stop worrying that he would lose his job for missing work. When his boss heard about Tommy's concern, he immediately called the hospital to leave a message that would reassure Tommy. He asked the nurse to tell Tommy to stop worrying and get better, that his job was waiting for him and that the entire crew sent their best wishes. Here is the message Tommy actually received:

Polk

Don't worry
about job
Phone call from
some man

Hardly a model of accuracy and completeness. And certainly not the comforting, caring message Tommy's boss intended.

Does it take longer to take a complete and meaningful message? Sometimes, but not that much longer. And if it's worth taking the message in the first place, it's worth doing it right.

WHAT INFORMATION TO INCLUDE

Standard message pads are useful because they prompt you to ask the right questions. But even without a form, you know what information is important and why. Just think about the information you would need if the message were meant for you.

• *The date and time of the message.* This information helps ensure that calls are returned promptly and that time isn't wasted responding to an old message.

• *The caller's full name.* It's tempting to just write "Bill," especially when callers say "Tell her Bill called." But unless you know for certain that she knows only one Bill, there is apt to be confusion. Ask, "May I have your last name, Bill?" It's also a good idea to verify spelling, too.

• *The company name and the caller's department.* It's easier to know who Bill is if the message receiver can put him into a context: "Oh, Bill Daniel is from Ajax, Inc. I placed a call to Sue at Ajax yesterday. He's in her department, so I'll bet he's following up on that call."

• *The phone number.* Make sure that you have the correct number by reading the number back to the caller *as you wrote it down.* Number transpositon—for instance, writing 6336 for 3636—happens in about 10 percent of messages. If you have a list of area codes handy (see Appendix B), it's helpful to note the state the caller is in if it is in a different time zone.

• *The message.* Does the caller need a call back? Or was

he asking to have information mailed or faxed to him? Is it urgent? When would be the best time to call?

• *Your name.* Just in case there is any uncertainty about the information you wrote down, give the message recipient a chance to ask you for clarification.

When you are the person leaving a message, help the message taker and the message recipient by giving conscious attention to these points of information.

KEEPING A PHONE LOG

A phone log is a listing of each incoming and/or outgoing call. It allows you to keep a record of, and to evaluate, how you are using the telephone. It also helps to ensure that you respond to each caller and that messages and requests don't fall through the cracks.

More and more, especially for legal and other professional services, it's important to be able to look back in the records and know who called whom, when, and why. Such information allows you to track progress in dealing with an ongoing customer problem or issue: "Yes, Ms. Winters, I can see on my phone log that you placed your order on the first of last month. I have a note that we shipped it via UPS. Since I have the date, I can easily track the shipment. May I call you back with my findings?"

Sometimes more than one person will be involved in solving a customer problem. Your phone log will provide continuity of information and a way for coworkers to know what action you've already taken. For example: "Mr. Schwartz, Juan Perez is out of the office today, but I see from his records that you called and spoke with him about this problem last Monday. After your call, he gave the necessary information to our billing department. You should be receiving the corrected invoice today. May I ask Mr. Perez to call you tomorrow to double check?"

Finally, in situations where disputes become potential legal battles, be aware that courts place considerable stock in phone logs as evidence of "the real story."

While there are many ways to keep a phone log—you can even buy special phone log books from office supply houses—the simple steno pad method as shown in Figure 2 works well. On the outside cover, record the starting and ending dates. Date the top of each page, and then use the space below to record your phone calls for that day. Or use one page to record phone calls over a period of several days. You can even tape or staple in messages that were taken for you. When a message or request has been handled, cross it out.

Figure 2.   Sample phone log page.

3/29 Peg Hamilton - ref. to ARTCO for salary data - (551) 555-1312

4/3 ARTCO- J. Miller will fax data on 3 industries phone w/ ? S

4/3 R. Jackson: wants "speech" on cust. fabk.-cb w/ dates & content ideas

4/5 Shipment not there! Hyatt Rm 210 Mary Clark - fedex ? How did we send this ??

4/5 Called M. Clark at hotel for details-cb when locate

When all the messages on the page have been taken care of, fold up the corner. That way, you'll be able to quickly flip through your book to find the work still to be done.

A FINAL MESSAGE ABOUT MESSAGES

Carol had been in a car accident. As the fifth vehicle in a five-car pile-up, her car was still drivable—but it wasn't pretty. Wanting to put the entire accident behind her, Carol was anxious to get the final damage estimate from her insurance agent and bring the car in for repair. After three weeks of "it's in the mail," an annoyed Carol called on a Friday afternoon and asked to speak directly to her agent.

"He's out until Monday," the receptionist explained.

"May I leave a message?"

"No, he doesn't want to come back to any messages. You'd better just call back on Monday." (CLICK.)

It's a true story. Carol went from annoyed to angry to the insurance company president.

To be effective, messages require cooperation between the message taker and the intended message receiver. Just as you take responsibility to take useful messages, take full responsibility to return messages.

CHAPTER 5

THE ART OF TRANSFERRING CALLS

No one *likes* to be transferred from Peter to Pammy to Pillar to Post and back again! So, whenever possible, help the caller yourself or take a message and have the appropriate person call back.

It's a good theory, but unless you "office alone," there will be times when you have to transfer a call, times when transferring allows you to serve the customer better than taking a message or helping yourself. There is an art to making that phone transfer smooth and effective that's not hard to learn.

A Five-Step Process for Transferring Calls

1. *Let the caller know that you are going to transfer the call.* There is little in this world as frustrating as being transferred against your will. Your customer may have a good reason for not wanting to be transferred, for example, "I'm calling from a pay phone at the airport, it took me ten minutes to get through, and I can't risk being cut off." The caller may have had a bad transfer experience with your company in the past, for example, "Every time I call, I just get transferred around, and I'm sick and tired of it." Whatever the case, respect your customer's feelings and help him or her to the best of your ability *without* making the transfer.

2. *Give the caller the name and phone number of the person you are transferring him or her to.* "I'm going to transfer you to Jill Applegate in billing. Her direct number is 555-5555."

If your main purpose in picking up a call is to transfer it, try substituting "How may I direct your call?" for "How may I help you?"

18

That way if there is any problem the caller will be able to get back to the right person.

3. *Preview the transfer process for the caller.* This is particularly important if you are transferring the customer into some type of automated call response system. "I'm transferring you to our automated billing department. There will be a few clicks and beeps and then you'll be asked to punch in your zip code. This will get you directly to a representative who will be able to pull your file right up and answer your questions." Without a preview, callers often hang up when transferred to an automated system.

4. *Thank the caller for allowing you to transfer the call.*

5. *If you can, stay on the line.* Explain why you've transferred the call and be sure you have directed the caller to the right person. Staying on the line also gives you a chance to save the call in case no one answers at the other end.

DEVELOP A CALL TRANSFER GUIDE

Unless you are a receptionist, chances are that most of the calls you transfer go to a limited number of people or departments. Rather than dig through the eight-pound company telephone book or rely on your own memory—"Was that extention 8734 or 7843?"—develop your own call transfer guide. Better yet, help lead an effort to develop one for use throughout your department or company.

A call transfer guide lists key topics and departments the way your *customer* asks about them. For example, in the newspaper business, advertising is divided into *contract advertising,* referring to the display ads that are contracted for by various businesses, and *noncontract advertising,* what people outside the industry call classified advertisements. Asking a customer who calls about placing an ad if he or she needs the contract or noncontract department is likely to create confusion. So, to be most effective, use the customer's language rather than industry jargon.

Sometimes call transfer guides list key individuals within departments and areas. If you do this, be especially vigilant about updating your guide. People tend to move more quickly than departments.

Your guide may be a single sheet of paper or several pages. The key is to keep it short enough to be quick and easy to use, yet complete enough to allow you to connect the caller with the right person or department.

CHAPTER 6

HOLD, PLEASE!

The average business person spends twenty-seven hours on hold each year.

—Communication Briefings, February 1991

You are entering a realm where time and space have no meaning. Where nothing is as it should be and where saying, "Will you hold, please?" has the power to make seconds become minutes and minutes become hours for another person, while the time just flies by for you.

Using the hold feature on your phone can be like sending the caller on a one-way trip to the Twilight Zone!

Why Use Hold?

There are a number of good reasons for engaging the hold button. You may have to answer a second line. You may have to leave your desk to get a piece of information. Or you may need a moment to regroup while handling an upset customer.

Do's and Don'ts to Keep You Out of the On-Hold Zone

- DO ask permission before placing the caller on hold. Then wait for and respect your customer's answer.
- DO tell the customer how long he or she should expect to be on hold.
- DON'T leave any caller on hold for more than thirty seconds without checking back, "Are you still able to hold?"
- DON'T use hold for more than three minutes with any caller.

- DON'T use hold when a call back will serve the customer equally well—and probably better.
- DO thank your customer for waiting!

THE SOUNDS OF SILENCE

To play hold music or not to play hold music—it can be an emotional issue! And there is no definitive answer. The best strategy is to keep customers off hold altogether, or on hold for only twenty seconds at a time, but that isn't always possible. For all of the complaining, studies suggest that callers who are on hold for more than one minute would rather have bad music than silence. At least with the music, callers know they are still connected. Silence leaves customers wondering if they are waiting for nothing.

To keep the process as painless and pleasant as possible, ask your customers what they would like to hear when they wait on hold: a particular type of music? local news? product information? Call your own phone line and *ask* to be put on hold. Do you like what you hear? Or has the tape become scratchy and annoying?

CHAPTER 7

GOTTA GET THAT OTHER LINE

Unless you have only one phone line without call waiting or are fortunate enough to always have an assistant or colleague who will handle the incoming calls, you will at times have to answer two—or more—lines at once. Guaranteed.

Juggling multiple phone lines can be the most stress-inducing aspect of using the telephone, especially when "receptionist" isn't part of your job description or of your training.

The good news is that almost anyone can—with a few pointers—handle more than one phone line in a way that leaves callers feeling good. (Though, if you need to handle six lines or more, or a real phone board, formal training is a must.)

Pointers for Handling More Than One Phone Line

1. If handling multiple calls isn't a regular part of your day—perhaps you are taking calls while coworkers are at lunch or at a meeting—*schedule your own business calls for another time.* Customers are far less willing to hold while you answer the second line if you called them in the first place.

2. Before you begin your duties as "temporary receptionist," find out if a coworker is expecting an important call. Know more about what's going on in your department or area than simply what is happening with your own job and your customers.

3. If you do need to place a call—or spend time with an incoming call—*be upfront about your situation.* Explain that

23

you are on phone duty and apologize *in advance* for any inconvenience this may cause.

4. When coworkers' phone lines are ringing through to your telephone, you may need to change the way you answer—instead of saying, "Hello, this is Mark," say "Hello, you've reached the Training Department."

5. If you pick up the second line only to take a message or to make a transfer, *make clear from the start what you can and cannot do*. A good way to do this is through your solicitation statement: "Hello, you've reached the Training Department. May I take a message or direct your call?" If you ask the usual question, "May I help you?" callers will begin to tell you about their needs or problems. And they will resent having their monologues interrupted with a hurried, "Look, I'm kinda busy with the phones and all. Can you make this quick or can I take a message?" or "That's Jane's area, but she's gone right now."

CHAPTER 8

CONFERENCE CALLING

You've seen the advertisements. Joe and Jane work at competing companies. Both have major deals to close. Their clients' executive teams are scattered at branch offices throughout the United States. Joe heads out to the airport. He flies to five cities in two days to meet face-to-face with each of the key decision makers. He's tired. He's rushed. His flight is cancelled, and he's history—while Jane sits comfortably in her own office, wrapping up the deal via a conference call with the client's CEO and the executive team.

Conference calling allows you to converse with three, four, five, or more people during a single phone call. Because long distance telephone rates are a lot cheaper than travel, conference calls appeal to the corporate bottom line. They can also lessen miscommunication and save time by ensuring that everyone hears the same message at the same time.

Unfortunately, many people find placing conference calls a daunting prospect. They don't have to be. In fact, most business phone systems (and an increasing number of home phones) come equipped with a conference calling feature. While you'll want to read the instructions for your own system (or look in your phone book), using your telephone's conference feature for a three-person call usually involves four steps:

1. Call the first party.
2. Ask him or her to hold.
3. Call the second party (often using a second phone line).
4. Push the CONFERENCE or ADD button and then reconnect with the person who is holding.

At the end, you'll have three people on the line (including yourself). Talk away!

If your telephone doesn't have a conference call feature, or if you need to add more than three individuals to the call, you can ask your local telephone company to create a conference call for you. Phone companies often refer to conference calls they set up as demand calls because the service is available to you "on demand."

Before requesting a demand call, have the names and phone numbers of all participants available. Call the operator at least ten minutes before you wish the conference call to begin. Give the operator the information, then hang up. The operator will call you back when he or she is ready to connect you to the conference call. Demand calls generally cannot be charged to a credit card or calling card. The phone company will bill the charges directly to your telephone number.

CONFERENCE CALL CAUTIONS

- **Be clear about who is supposed to call whom. It's frustrating when each person sits around waiting for the other people to call.**
- **Be clear about the time of the call, especially when the conference call will cross time zones. Will the call take place at 3:00 P.M. Eastern or Pacific time?**
- **If an operator is connecting the call, be prepared to wait on the line while the operator contacts the other participants. It can take as long as one minute for each caller, so you could wait five minutes for a five-party call to be connected.**
- **Know what to do if one party is accidently disconnected. Can you reconnect the call through your phone system? Who will call the conference call operator and request a reconnect call?**

CHAPTER 9

ANSWERING MACHINES AND VOICE MAIL—AND OTHER POTENTIAL TECHNOLOGICAL NIGHTMARES

Telephone technology has come a long way since the days of Alexander Graham Bell. And each new innovation in telecommunication has raised questions—and eyebrows. For every person who embraces a new piece of technology as a new sign of progress, another expresses dismay that high-tech is again replacing high-touch.

"IF YOU'D LIKE TO LEAVE A MESSAGE . . ."

How many of your friends who swore they would never have an answering machine—"If people want to talk with me they can just call back"—now can't live without one? Probably more than a few. Whether you are using the old-fashioned answering machine or today's voice mail or voice messaging, a few tips will keep the system working for you and for your customers.

1. *Change your message daily*. If you won't be able to return calls before 4:00 P.M., say so.
2. *Don't use a "cute" announcement unless it's appropriate to your business*. "Hello. You've reached the Black and White Photo Studio. Please tell us your name, number, and the time you called—we hate to be kept in the dark!"

3. *Offer an alternative number.* Give your customer a chance to talk with someone else, a real human, if the need is immediate.
4. *Indicate the type of message that should be left.* If you are using an answering machine, chances are you will have to ask callers to leave relatively brief messages. A voice mail system, on the other hand, may allow callers to leave long and complicated messages. If your system doesn't indicate the time of the call, ask the caller to provide this information.
5. *Listen to your own message periodically to make sure that it is clear and that the system is working properly.* Message tapes don't last forever. Depending upon usage and tape quality, you should change your incoming and outgoing message tapes at least four times a year (and perhaps as often as once a month).

When you *leave* a message on voice mail or an answering machine, give your name and number first. That way if the time allowed for messages is short—seven to ten seconds—the critical information will be there.

PAGERS AND BEEPERS

Pagers and beepers are a terrific way to allow your customers or coworkers to contact you when you aren't near a telephone. They have traditionally been provided to employees who spend large amounts of time at their customers' places of business, for example, service technicians or sales professionals. Pagers and beepers have also given companies and customers a way to contact key employees in case of after-hours emergencies. More and more, personal pagers and beepers are being used to replace public address paging systems when employees are in the building but not tied to a desk.

The frustration with pagers and beepers occurs when their function is misunderstood or they are used poorly. Robert Weiss, sales manager for American Paging of Minnesota, offers these tips for effective pager use:

1. Know why an employee is carrying a pager or a beeper before you use it to contact him or her, or give the number to a customer. If the pager is there for emergencies only, know what constitutes an emergency and don't use the number for nonemergency situations.

2. If you have a pager, carry it with you at all times. Pagers can't connect you to customers when they are left on your car visor or on top of your dresser.

3. Wear or carry your pager as intended, usually on a belt or attached to a purse. Pagers get lost or are easily stolen when users don't attach them as recommended.

4. Let the people who will be calling you on your pager know how long it usually takes you to return a call. It's professional and courteous, and it will help eliminate unnecessary duplicate pages.

5. Before you give a pager number to a customer, explain the type of message the pager will accept. Different types of pagers can take different types of messages. Some only allow you to send a phone number. Others will accept a voice message. The newest pagers will accept a text message that is transmitted by the sender.

Thirty percent of callers hang up when they encounter automated response systems.

—ANDREW LUPTON CEO, U.S. Message Corp.

AUTOMATIC CALL PROCESSING

Sometimes called voice processing, automatic call processing can improve the flow of communication by taking some of the human connections out of the customer contact process. Used well, it can bind together customer service reps, tele-

**CAUTION:
Automatic
call sys-
tems only
work with
touch tone
dialing. And
not every
customer
who has
traded in an
old rotary
phone for a
push button
model actu-
ally has
touch tone
dialing.
When that's
the case,
know what
number cus-
tomers can
call to by-
pass the
system and
talk directly
to a human
being.**

phone systems, and computer databases so that questions can be answered and problems solved with a single phone call. In addition, automatic processing may allow customer service reps to spend longer periods of time dealing with unusual customer requests and problem solving.

Call processing systems take customers through a series of push button steps until they get the information they want or are connected to a human. A survey conducted by *Bank Administration* magazine found that 70 percent of the banks surveyed had installed a voice response system, offering customers the opportunity to check their balance, find out if a particular check has cleared, and transfer funds between accounts via their telephone.

SPEAKER PHONES

Remember when you were a child and made your own telephone by poking holes in the bottoms of two soup cans and tying them together with a string? You had to yell to be heard, and the sound was fuzzy and distorted, yet the crude technology you used as a budding inventor probably provided more clarity than most of today's speaker phones.

So, before you use a speaker phone, ask yourself, "Is this really necessary? Is it adding something to the conversation?"

People often turn to speaker phones when a temporary physical limitation—a sprained wrist, for example—makes holding the handset difficult or impossible, or when it's necessary to move around the office and still continue the conversation. However, a headset is a better long-term solution for both of these situations. The best reason for using a speaker phone is that it allows you to involve two or more people in the conversation at your end without setting up a formal telephone conference call.

But no matter when or why you use your speaker phone, keep two courtesy tips in mind:

1. *Consider the people around you.* Speaker phones can be loud. If you are talking into yours from across the office, you may be loud, too. So, make sure you shut your door (if you have one) and are sensitive to the needs of those who have offices around you.

2. *Respect your customer's privacy.* If you are using your speaker phone so that someone else can hear the conversation, introduce that person at the start— even if he or she won't be taking an active role in the discussion.

CHAPTER 10

TEXT TELEPHONES: CUSTOMERS CAN SEE WHAT YOU'RE SAYING

The Americans with Disabilities Act (ADA) brings a new sensitivity to customers and employees with disabilities. About 9 percent of Americans are deaf or hard-of-hearing. As access improves and barriers are removed, you will interact with more and more such individuals as customers and coworkers.

Most people with full hearing are unfamiliar with the special needs of the deaf and hearing-impaired community. You may even find the prospect of communicating with a customer with a hearing impairment somewhat daunting. Don't worry—it's easy.

THE TEXT TELEPHONE

Until 1964, telephones were for the hearing community alone. If you were deaf, you needed to rely on a friend or neighbor to place your calls. It was in 1964 that deaf scientist Robert Weitbrecht invented a way for people to use teletypewriters (TTYs) to communicate with each other over the telephone. If you use a computer, you may have used Weitbrecht's invention—the modem.

Over the years the technology has changed. And so, too, has the terminology. The FCC recently declared *text telephone* (TT) to be the preferred term, but many people still refer to telephone devices for the deaf as TDDs (telephone devices for the deaf) or TTYs.

A text telephone is simply a telephone that is attached (either by cable or as a single unit) to a keyboard. The message typed on the keyboard is transmitted via a modem to a second text telephone, where it is displayed on a screen. Some text telephones are equipped with printers that allow the sender or receiver to keep a copy of the conversation. The abbreviation TT, TTD, or TTY before or after a telephone number indicates that the number connects to a text telephone (i.e., 555-5555 [TT], or 555-5555 [V/TT] for a number that connects to both voice and text telephone service).

Several other types of equipment may be used by hearing-impaired customers. Telephone amplifiers, which attach to regular telephones, make the incoming voice louder. Ring signalers indicate a ringing telephone through flashing lights, vibrating wrist bands, or by changing the ring to a sound that is more easily heard. Special large visual displays or braille units are often attached to TTs for individuals with sight impairment.

RELAY SERVICES

As of July 1993, all companies offering telephone service to the general public are required to offer telephone relay services to individuals who use telecommunications devices for the deaf. By using a relay service, you can communicate with a customer who is deaf even if you don't have a TT, provided that your customer does. Relay operators keep all calls 100 percent confidential.

Use your local phonebook to find the number of the relay service in your area, and post it with your other important phone numbers.

PLACING A RELAY SERVICE CALL

Have your customer's phone number ready before you call the relay operator. If the call is long distance, be prepared to tell the operator which long distance company you wish to use. If you have a calling card number, have that ready, too.

Relay operators may be busy, so stay on the line if it rings without answering (that means you are in the queue) or call back if the number is busy. You may want to ask your local relay service to suggest the best times for you to call.

TTs can handle conversations of about sixty typed words per minute, so know what you need to say and how you will say it (see the box for commonly used TT abbreviations). Operators are in demand, so you will want to keep to the point. You can expect your TT conversations to take about four times as long as comparable voice conversations.

If your relay call reaches an answering machine or voice mail box, the relay operator may hang up and then ask you if you want to leave a message. If you do, the operator will redial and leave your message. Be sure to include the number of the relay service in the message you leave.

TT ETIQUETTE

Incoming TT calls are sometimes hard to identify. Many of the older machines make a high-pitched series of tones (similar to many fax machines), and many of the newer ones

TT ABBREVIATIONS

GA	**"Go ahead."**
Q	**Question mark**
PLS HD	**"Please hold."**
U	**"You"**
R	**"Are"**
SK	**"Stop keying." Indicates that the conversation is at an end.**

Punctuation is often not used. A space indicates the end of a sentence.

> **You *can* use words like *see* and *hear* with people who are blind or deaf.**
>
> —DR. CHADA
> MALOFF,
> *Business and*
> *Social*
> *Etiquette with*
> *Disabled People*

make no sound at all. Consequently, TT callers are hung up on a lot. (A few machines have a synthesized voice which will inform you that the caller has a hearing impairment.) If your company offers TT phone numbers, be aware that a silent call may be a misdirected call.

When calling a person with a hearing impairment, let the phone ring longer than usual. Be extra careful about distracting background noises—computer printers, office chatter—that may make it difficult for your customer to hear you. Pause after each sentence to be sure your customer is following the conversation.

Because there is no voice to recognize with TTs, it is extremely important that at the beginning of your message you identify yourself and your reason for calling. If you are using a TT yourself and make a typing error, don't bother to correct it as long as the word can be understood. If you need to place the other party on hold, be certain that you type "PLS HD."

To end the conversation, both parties say or type their goodbyes, ending with "SK," before hanging up. Frequently, both parties will conclude by typing "SKSK."

Resources

For more information on text telephone, contact:

National Center for Law and
   the Deaf
Gallaudet University
800 Florida Avenue N.E.
Washington, D.C. 20002-
   3265
202-651-5373 (V/TT)

Telecommunications for the
   Deaf, Inc.
814 Thayer Avenue
Silver Spring, Md. 20910
301-589-3786 (V)
301-589-3006 (TT)

Tele-Consumer Hotline
1910 K St. N.W.
Suite 610
Washington, D.C. 20006
800-332-1124 (V/TT)
202-223-4371 (V/TT)

CHAPTER 11

A FEW WORDS
ABOUT PHONE FRAUD

The telephone is a wonderful invention, a positive tool for business and personal use. Unfortunately, not everyone who uses the telephone is as honest and scrupulous as you. It's important to think about phone fraud because you, and your company, may be victimized by it. It's also important because phone fraud artists, mimicking the services and products you provide, may victimize your customers. And that makes it all the harder for honest folks to do business via the telephone.

TONER BANDITS AND
OTHER SHADY DEALERS

Phone scams are popular with businesses and with individual consumers. An old standby is the "toner bandit" and its many variations. The scam works in three stages:

1. The bandit learns what type of copier equipment (or fax machine, or typewriter, or other equipment) your company uses, and the name of the person in charge of ordering supplies.

2. The bandit calls, usually identifying him- or herself as "from the warehouse," and tells you that "there is going to be a big price jump, and I knew you would want to stock up on toner for your Minolta 450Z before that happens." Whether or not the bandit actually breaks the law at this point (by misrepresenting him- or herself as your regular

36

supplier) really doesn't matter. If you fall for the call, you will place an order *as if* you were talking to your regular (and honest!) supplier. Because you *think* you're talking to the "good guys," you won't check and see that this "special sale price" is actually several times what you normally pay.

3. The bandit collects your order and your money. And you are left with some *very expensive* toner.

More recent entrants into the phone fraud field are chargeable call scams. Chargeable calls—those 900 numbers where the caller pays a fee when the call is placed, and often a per-minute charge—have changed the meaning of telephone service. There are legitimate chargeable call numbers for everything from sports scores and recipes to fantasy fulfillment.

The most recent scam is getting you to place the call without your realizing there is a fee—until you get your phone bill. This grew from the fact that demand for 900 numbers has outstripped supply so that telephone companies are now issuing chargeable call numbers without the telltale 900 area code or prefix. Bandits using this scam call business numbers (especially pager numbers) and leave a message that says only "Call me at *###-###-####*." Not wanting to miss a customer, you return the call, only to have a fee charged to your phone bill. It's not illegal—yet. But it's definitely not nice.

It's important to know that the bandits are out there—selling everything from toner to light bulbs—making life a little harder for the rest of us. If bandits operate in your industry, show your customers how to avoid their phone fraud tactics. And keep a wary eye out for yourself and your company, too.

PART

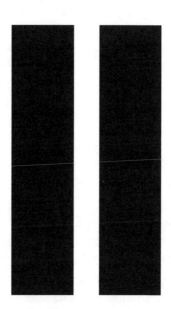

MANAGING YOUR CALL

Managing your call means paying attention both to the technology of telephone communication and to the psychology of the person on the other end of the line. Because the telephone physically changes your communication with others, it is particularly critical that you actively shape—that is, actively manage—your service on the line.

Managing your call starts before you pick up the phone to place a call or answer an insistent ring, and it doesn't stop until after you've replaced the handset and broken the connection. It involves considering what you want to say and then consciously choosing the words and strategy you will use to communicate your message over the telephone. The words you choose, and the vocal tone with which you say them, will determine whether you communicate clearly or get a dead line.

CHAPTER 12

PUTTING YOUR BEST VOICE FORWARD: EFFECTIVE TELEPHONE GREETINGS

Creating a positive first impression begins before you even pick up the phone. It starts with finishing your previous call or conversation. Sound too obvious? It's surprising how many phone calls begin with a click as the handset is lifted, and the shadow of a voice at some distance saying ". . . so I told him that just wasn't the way things worked around here. Well, anyway, gotta get this call." Then a pause. And then, finally, "Hello, XYZ Company. How may I help you?"

Separate each phone call, physically and emotionally. Your customer doesn't know, and probably doesn't care, whether the previous caller infuriated you or left you laughing hysterically. Start *this* call on an even emotional keel.

Effective greetings contain three elements: a salutation, an identification statement, and a solicitation of information

ELEMENTS OF AN EFFECTIVE GREETING

Salutation: "Good morning," "Good evening," or "Hello"

Identification: "This is Ms. Polsky" or "You've reached XYZ Company"

Solicitation: "How may I help you?" or "How may I direct your call?"

from the caller. The salutation does two things. First, it sets a friendly tone. Second, because phone systems sometimes cut off the first word or syllable you say, it protects the more important identification statement.

The identification statement simply lets the caller know what department or individual he or she has reached. Here are some examples:

- Use your *company* name when calls are most frequently from external customers who may or may not have contacted you in the past.
- Use your *department* when calls frequently come from external customers or employees using a general departmental number.
- Use your *name* when calls come most frequently from external customers or coworkers who are using your direct phone number.

If callers are split between those wanting to reach anyone in your department or area and those who wish to reach you specifically, it may be helpful to use two identification statements: "Hello, you've reached Ron [*identification statement 1*] in the Training Department [*identification statement 2*]." That

WARM UP YOUR VOICE

Just as you stretch your legs before you run your first lap, you need to stretch your voice before you take your first call. Here's an old favorite: "To sit in solemn silence on a dull dark dock, in a pestilential prison with a life long lock, awaiting the sensation of a short sharp shock, from a cheap and chippy chopper on a big black block." Say it slow, then fast, first with your deepest voice, then in your highest. Have fun with it!

way, your greeting provides the needed information to both types of callers.

The solicitation statement asks customers to tell you how you may be of service. If your role is primarily to transfer callers to other departments or individuals, narrow your solicitation statement to "How may I direct your call?"

CHAPTER 13

WHEN YOU HAVE TO SCREEN CALLS

"Hello, you've reached the office of Mr. Untouchable. How may I help you?"

"Mr. Untouchable, please."

"And you are? . . ."

"Mr. Gotaproblem. I'm a customer of his."

"Well, you *aren't* on my list."

With experiences like that, it's not surprising callers resist being screened. Screening can make the "protected" party appear pretentious and customers feel that you don't think they are important. In fact, screening sometimes gets such a strong negative reaction that it's tempting to declare a moratorium on all call screening. Yet, there are times when it is necessary for you to screen calls for someone you work for or with.

Before you choose your screening tactic, have a clear understanding of what the person you are screening needs:

- Are there callers who should *always* be put through?
- Might someone call in relation to the project at hand?
- Are there callers who should *never* be put through?
- Is the person you are screening calls for expecting certain calls?
- When should you report on the messages you take—as they occur or at certain times during the day?
- When should you tell callers that their calls will be returned?

Screening may be required because a coworker is on a tight deadline and can spend time only on key calls or on those related to the project at hand. In that case, use *Screening Tactic 1:* Take a Message. The easiest way to keep callers from feeling that their call doesn't pass the importance test is to take messages from all callers. Then use your prescreening information to prioritize the messages.

The information you gather when screening calls can give your coworker a chance to focus on the purpose of the call before being connected with the caller—"Joan Gates called about the latest sale catalog. She thinks there's a pricing error on page 47."

Screening calls also allows you to identify which questions or problems are better handled by yourself, or by some other staff member. To do this, use *Screening Tactic 2:* "Will She/He Know What This Is in Regard To?" Asking this question should get most callers to open up to you about the purpose of their call without feeling defensive. As you listen, you'll be able to assess whether or not the caller would be better served by you or if the caller should be put through as originally requested.

Finally, screening calls allows you to weed out unwanted and unannounced sales calls. When you screen an unexpected sales call, use *Screening Tactic 3:* Ask for It in Writing. Don't be surprised if Screening Tactics 1 or 2 surface a cold sales call. And don't be annoyed. Sales calls are a terrific way to learn about new products and services. But that doesn't mean that you have to drop everything to listen to the pitch. When using Tactic 3, explain that while Mr. or Ms. Too Busy is unable to take the call, you'd be happy to direct written information to his or her attention. If the salesperson isn't willing to write, then you probably aren't missing much. If the salesperson follows through, his or her material deserves a review.

CHAPTER 14

KEEPING YOUR FEET ON THE FLOOR (AND OUT OF YOUR MOUTH)

The words come out of your mouth, just as your foot works its way in—"She had to go and took the *Journal* with her. It could be a while." You can't stop them, and you can't unsay them. Fortunately, you can prevent them by thinking *in advance* about the words you will—and won't—use to ensure that your message hits the mark.

To avoid misinterpretation, and possible bad feelings, think before you initiate a joke or a laugh with a caller. Are you 100 percent certain the caller will see the humor in the situation? Avoid jargon the customer may not understand. If the customer refers to your product as the C&J767/K, fine. You can, too. But don't begin with the "tech talk."

Never speak disparagingly of your coworkers or your company. When the customer calls, you are the company. The caller doesn't care about your internal company problems. If your company is suffering some internal malady, beware that you don't give the impression that you *could* say a lot, but are holding back.

DO Say	**DON'T Say**
After Answering/Placing a Call	
"Thanks for returning my call!"	"It sure took you long enough. Why didn't you call sooner?"

DO Say	DON'T Say
"It's so nice to talk with you again."	"Aren't you the lady with the really dumb complaint?"
"Do you have a moment?" or "Is now a good time?"	"We need to talk right this minute." (Unless it really *is* an emergency.)

When Taking/Leaving a Message

"May I take your number (or leave my number) for quick reference?"	"Of course he has my number—I'm returning his call."
"She's not in her office (or not available) at the moment."	"She went to buy another candy bar." (The caller doesn't need to know where she went or why.)
"She's off site (or working out of the office) this week."	"She's out of the state on vacation." (Whether it's play time or work time, it's a bad idea to tell callers that a coworker is on the road.)

When Probing for Information

"Will there be anything else?"	"Are you through yet?" or "Is that it?"
"I don't mean to sound uninformed, can you tell me more about this?"	"Well, *I* never heard of anything like that before." (Implying the caller made it up.) Or, worse yet, "Sir that's just not possible."

When Assisting a Customer

"It will be my pleasure."	"No problem." (That implies that it normally would be a problem.)

DO Say	DON'T Say
"I suggest you . . ." or "I'd like to ask you to . . ." or "I think the best way (or the fastest way) to handle this would be . . ."	"You'll have to . . ." or "You'll need to . . ."
"Here's what I can do for you."	"We can't do that." Or "It's company policy, so what can I do?"
"The person who handles that is _____. Let me get her on the line." (Or some other action that will involve her in assisting the caller.)	"It's not my job."
"Let me find that information for you."	"I don't know."
"May I . . ." or "Please . . ."	Just transfer or put the customer on hold.

Anytime

"I'm so glad you called." Or "Thank you." Or "You're very welcome."	"Are we through yet?"
The customer's name (the way he or she wishes it to be used).	"Honey" or "Lady" or "Buddy."

CHAPTER 15

PLANNING AHEAD

The best way to use the telephone efficiently, in order to avoid wasting your time or your customer's time, is to plan your call before you place it. Even if most of your calls are incoming, you can still plan them. Just think in terms of the most frequent reasons customers call.

Chances are you will be able to group most of your customer calls into a few broad categories: assistance with a problem, information on products and services, to take advantage of special promotions and offers, to place orders.

Planning is an easy, five-step process. It can be formalized into a script, jotted down as a few notes on a Post-It, or simply a thought process you go through before you dial. Choose the method that works best for you. The Sample Telephone Planning Guide on pages 50–51 outlines the key points you will want to consider before placing your call. Note that the planning process doesn't follow the same chronological order as the actual phone call. Instead, planning begins with understanding the heart of your message and then working from there.

(Text continues on page 52.)

Telephone Time = Your Customer's Time
+ Your Company's Time
+ Your Time.
Don't Waste It.

SAMPLE TELEPHONE PLANNING GUIDE

Customer:

Open:
How can I begin this phone call effectively?

Purpose:
What does this call need to accomplish?

In order to achieve my purpose, what is the most important point for me to communicate?

What information supports that point?
1.

2.

In order to achieve my purpose, what is the second most important point?

What information supports that point?
1.

2.

Close:
How can I end this call most effectively?

Questions:

What questions might your customer ask you?

Objections:

What objections might your customer raise? Objections to the product? The service? The timing?

Call Review:

What worked well during the call? What can you do to be better during the next call?

The Five-Step Planning Process

1. *Identify the purpose of the call.* Just what do you want to accomplish through this call? Make a sale? Give information? Get information? Set up an appointment? What does your customer want to accomplish through this call?

2. *Identify topic areas.* Decide what areas you need to talk about or what information you need to offer in order to accomplish your purpose. This will keep you from getting sidetracked. In general, you will want to focus on only two or three specific areas, with about two subpoints under each.

Keep in mind that your telephone call should be kept short and to the point. To get customers to do what you want, you need to stress how that action will benefit them.

3. *Identify potential questions and objections.* Your customer may ask you to explain some things in more detail or question the validity of the information you offer. If you are making a sales call, your customer may want to discuss a competitor's product, or offer reasons why now is not a good time to buy. The more you can anticipate and plan, the better able you will be to respond effectively.

4. *Develop an opening and a closing.* Most people want to start here, but your opening and closing should be the last thing you think about. Only after you have a clear idea of your main objective and how you plan to achieve it can you choose the most effective way of beginning and closing the telephone call.

5. *Review.* After you complete a call, review it. What worked well? And what didn't? Did the customer raise a question or objection that you hadn't thought of? If so, add it to your script/note.

Planning your telephone calls is an ongoing process. Continue to do it, and you'll improve your ability to communicate effectively and efficiently over the telephone.

CHAPTER 16

ASKING QUESTIONS

Callers don't know what you need to know until you tell them.

Simple? Maybe. Of the way we communicate day-to-day, ~~55~~ 60 percent (the nonverbal part) is missing in telephone conversations. So, you just about have to be Sherlock Holmes to ferret out and follow up on the important clues you do get about what customers want and need, and about the way they feel. It can be a tough job!

In telephone conversations, you will use three types of questions:

1. Background questions
2. Probing questions
3. Confirming questions

Background questions are those that help you direct a caller to the proper person or department, or that allow you to pull up a customer's profile or account. Probing questions help you delve into a customer problem or complaint, to identify the real issue and the best solution. Confirming questions provide a system of checks and balances. They help you verify that you've correctly understood the customer's message.

BACKGROUND QUESTIONS

Customers sometimes resist background questions. They want to talk about their problem or question and may not understand why you are asking for their Social Security number and mother's maiden name.

If a customer is upset and needs to vent, you may need to listen for a while (taking notes!) before asking your background questions. It's a good idea to preview this stage of the conversation by saying something like, "I appreciate your concern, Ms. Customer. If you will help me with a bit more information, I'll get you connected to an agent right away." The preview reassures your customer that you do care and that the background questions do have a purpose.

PROBING QUESTIONS

Probing questions help you to gather information about the problem at hand. The exact questions you ask will vary with the situation (be sure to refer back to the notes you took when your customer was venting!), but a good place to start is with the five W's: who, what, when, where, and why.

Probing questions should invite the customer to offer more than "yes" and "no" answers. Other probing questions include the following:

> "Could you tell me more about that?"
> "What happened next?"
> "What do you need to happen now?"
> "Could you give me an example?"

Remember that during probing you are asking for information, not evaluating or challenging it. An upset customer may talk in extremes—"I must have called a hundred times and no one ever called me back." Don't get caught up in the customer's hyperbole. Instead, look for the core issue—the customer called at least once and never got a call back. That's important information.

CONFIRMING QUESTIONS

Silence on the other end of the line isn't necessarily evidence of customer agreement. Silence frequently signals that the customer has given up on making you understand, or is frustrated or angry, or that he or she is embarrassed to admit confusion. Confirming questions help you to know what your customer is thinking when he or she doesn't offer vocal feedback.

Confirming questions include:

"So, what you are saying is . . ."
"How am I doing with my explanation? Am I helping or did I miss the point of your question?
"How do you feel about the solution I suggested?"

Confirming questions may be the most difficult to ask because the *tone* you use is so important. It is frighteningly easy to ask "Do you understand?" in such a way that your customer *hears,* "Only an idiot wouldn't understand this. Are you an idiot?" The problem is that you and I don't intend to send that message at all. It just comes out. To prevent it, listen to yourself and assess your own vocal tone. And listen when others ask you confirming questions. What phrasing and vocal tone communicates genuine concern? Work to use that same phrasing and tone in your telephone conversations.

CHAPTER 17

MAKING A SHOW OF LISTENING

The listening process is a combination of what we hear, what we understand, and what we remember. When you listen well, you learn more. When you make your listening process visible to your customer, you communicate respect and caring. By so doing, you say, "I think you are important. I value what you are telling me."

GOOD LISTENING IS LEARNED

Hearing is a physical ability. It is what happens when sound waves vibrate your ear drum and that signal is transmitted via the auditory nerve to the brain. Listening is not a physical ability. Nor is it tied to intelligence; some of the world's smartest people are poor listeners. They think listening well is letting the other person talk before getting to the real heart of the matter—when *they* get to talk! Listening is a skill, and like any other skill, it can be learned and improved with practice. To improve your listening, make a point of listening to difficult material (I like to listen to National Press Club speeches broadcast on public radio), and take notes about the content. Practice listening for key points and ideas. It will help you learn how to listen better to your own customers.

While we generally speak at 125 to 150 words per minute, we can listen and understand more than *400 words* per minute. Use your mental quickness wisely. Carefully consider the information your customer is giving you, review the content mentally, and listen for additional meaning.

You can actually improve your interest in listening by seeking out personal benefits: If I listen well, I may learn new information; if I listen well, my customer will be more open to my suggestions; if I listen well, I will be able to offer exactly what my customer needs. As your interest in listening well increases, so too will your concentration and learning.

Improving listening also means identifying and eliminating any bad habits you may have acquired. Below is a list of five of the most common poor listening habits. How many have you been guilty of? How many have you encountered when trying to communicate with someone else?

The Five Most Common Poor Listening Habits

HOW SOON WE FORGET After 1 day we forget 46 percent of what we've heard. After 7 days we forget 65 percent of what we've heard. After 14 days we forget 79 percent of what we've heard.

—H. F. SPITZER, researcher

1. *Interruptions.* They say to the customer, "What you have to say isn't very important to me." Do you go through unrelated files or type on your computer during phone conversations with customers? Do co-workers feel free to ask you questions or interrupt while you're on the phone?
2. *Fear of not having all the answers.* You don't need to know all the answers to be a good listener. This bad habit can cause you to miss the real questions, and sometimes what the speaker really wants isn't answers but understanding.
3. *Believing that you know better than the speaker does.* This habit can cause you to dismiss the customer's message, or even to interrupt it with a premature solution.
4. *Overreacting.* When something a customer says pushes one of your "hot buttons"—perhaps you are offended by the customer's choice of language or style of explanation—it's easy to stop listening. Instead, you begin mentally disagreeing—saying in your mind what you would like to say out loud.
5. *Pseudolistening.* Often listeners just pretend to listen, whereas in reality they are focusing their attention somewhere else.

MAKE THE PROCESS VISIBLE

In face-to-face communication, it's easy to give nonverbal clues and verbal feedback that show that you are listening. You probably learned to do that in your earliest years when your parents demanded special listening behaviors—"Look at me when I'm speaking to you." On the telephone, it's much harder. You must rely on the words you use, the questions you ask, and the "uh huh"s and "mmm"s that replace head nodding and gestures.

CHAPTER 18

WHEN YOU HAVE TO SAY "NO"

The Golden Rule of Service: Great service is something you do *with* and *for* customers, never *to* them.

It's a mistake to think that good service means always saying "yes" to customers and coworkers. Sometimes the best, and most helpful, thing you can do for a caller is to say "no."

The old model of good service was that of master and servant, with the servant—the person performing the service—simply following orders and doing whatever the master—the customer—wanted. That model no longer works.

Today's service model centers on *partnership,* on customers and service professionals working together to meet and exceed needs.

A key element of partnership is openness and honesty. You rely on your customer to share with you his or her wants and needs. And your customer relies on you to know what you can and cannot do to fulfill those needs.

It's easy to work with your caller when the answer is "yes, it will be my pleasure." Getting around "no," while maintaining your partnership relationship, is far more challenging. Here are three ways to meet the challenge:

1. *Don't assume you can't.* Partners are willing to seek creative and innovative solutions. Before you say you can't, work with your customer to try to find a way that you can.

2. *Find an alternative.* While you may not be able to do exactly what your customer is requesting—"I'm sorry, but I need to get my manager's approval before I can reverse those bank charges"—you may be able to do something else that is just as good—"What I can do is put a hold on those

59

charges so they won't affect your balance until I talk with my manager and check back with you. Will that be satisfactory?"

3. *Focus on the positive.* The positives reinforce the relationship. Begin and end every "no" with a positive, such as "I really appreciate your bringing this to my attention," or "I can understand your concern," or "The information you gave me will help us to make improvements. I'll be sure to relate your concerns at the next staff meeting (or to the appropriate person)."

CHAPTER 19

IN CASE OF EMERGENCY!

It is to be hoped that you will never be in a situation where you need to contact the fire or police departments or summon emergency medical assistance. But it is better to think about it now, rather than wonder "What should I do?" if the situation does arise.

CALL FOR HELP

Most communities in the United States now have 911 access to emergency services. Find out if you can dial 911 directly from your company phone system. Many phone systems that can be programmed to allow 911 direct dialing (including private pay phones) aren't, simply because no one thought of doing it—until someone needed to make that call.

If your community doesn't have 911, or if you need to use a different number to access the system through your office telephone, post the emergency number *on every phone*.

When you call, try to remain calm. The operator will need to know the following:

- The nature of the problem
- Where you are located
- Your name

The operator may ask you to stay on the line while he or she calls the appropriate emergency services. By staying on the line, you can keep the operator—and the emergency professionals who are en route to help you—apprised of any changes in the situation.

WHAT TO DO NEXT

While your first concern will be to get trained professionals on the scene as needed (paramedics, firefighters, police),

---

IN CASE OF EMERGENCY!

Emergency Service Numbers:

Fire Department   _____

Medical Assistance   _____

Police   _____

Company Emergency Numbers:

Nurse   _____

Security   _____

Human Resources   _____

Staff Who Know CPR

_____

Ext. _____

_____

Ext. _____

_____

Ext. _____

_____

Ext. _____

company officials will also want to know about the situation, even if it is minor. Find out if there is a company or departmental policy for handling emergencies. If not, help to design one. The procedure may be different for medical emergencies and for police- and fire-related emergencies.

AFTER THE EMERGENCY IS OVER

Once you've had a chance to collect yourself, take a sheet of paper and outline what happened and what was done. Don't worry about making it neat or using complete sentences. Just get it written down. Emergencies are by nature stressful, and our memories of them can quickly become fuzzy and incomplete. The notes you take while it is still fresh in your mind will help you and your company know how well your emergency procedures worked, and this will help you improve them for the next time.

CHAPTER 20

TELEPHONE SELLING

Caught you! You were going to skip this one because selling isn't part of your job description. It doesn't matter. What you'll learn here *will* help you in your job. After all, *everyone* does some selling over the phone—even if it is only selling the caller on the idea that you have the necessary information or that you are capable of taking the requested message.

Telephone selling has gotten a bad reputation with many people. Who hasn't been called away from the dinner table to listen to "a fabulous, once in a lifetime chance to . . .?" You get the picture.

But professional telephone selling should really be called "sharing information and alternatives." Remember, you and your customer are partners. Even if the call you are placing is "cold" (i.e., you are calling a prospect who has not done business with you before), you've already determined that what you have to offer will be of potential benefit and interest to your customer. What you are doing in your call is sharing that information, offering your product or service as an alternative to the product or service the prospect is currently using—or doing without.

Benefits of Selling by Phone

1. Tough-to-contact people are often more willing to give you fifteen minutes for a phone call, than to schedule a face-to-face meeting—where, they fear, thirty minutes might turn into (or seem like) hours.
2. You can take notes, refer to job aids or notes, and use a script without distracting the customer.

64

3. The telephone commands attention and privacy. When the phone rings, isn't your first reaction to answer it? This is a plus for telephone selling—provided that you don't *abuse* it. People also tend to be more candid on the phone. Think about it—talking on the telephone can be like talking in the dark. It has a certain feel of anonymity.

4. The telephone has immediacy. On the telephone, it is easier to come to the point and ask for action without your customer feeling rushed.

To warm yourself up to the job of cold calling, focus on three things: (1) understanding the odds; (2) developing your skills; and (3) self-motivation.

THE ODDS

Before you begin teleselling, whether you are making cold calls or suggesting product add-ons, understand that *no one* has a 100 percent success rate. In fact, many experts believe that a 4:1 ratio of tries to buys is evidence of superior skill and performance.

THE SKILLS

Many of the skills you use in teleselling are the same as those you use in any other telephone conversation: Listening, voice control (you'll learn more about this in Chapter 23), a good telephone personality, and preplanning your call are all important.

If you use a script, it will be especially important to keep your voice conversational. Avoid reading in a monotone. And remember that customers don't know *their* lines—they won't always provide the target response to your questions.

Be prepared to go "off script," to answer unexpected customer questions or to respond to comments.

In addition, you will want to develop a recordkeeping or feedback system to track how you are doing and to identify techniques that work well. If your company doesn't have a standard feedback sheet, consider developing your own, or use the Telephone Prospecting Score Sheet below. The score sheet is a simple way for you tick off the number of calls you make each day, whether the call actually gets through (contacts)—and if so, how the customer responded—or if the call went unanswered or was a wrong number.

TELEPHONE PROSPECTING SCORE SHEET

Date						
Calls Made						
Contacts						
Yes						
No						
???						
No Answer						
Busy						
Wrong Number						
Wrong Person						

Copyright 1992 Performance Research Associates, Inc.

SELF-MOTIVATION

It's tough to keep yourself up when customers keep turning you down—even when you know the odds. Give yourself a break, literally, by scheduling rewards for a job well done. For example, after ten calls get a fresh cup of coffee. Or, after five calls put the phone down, shut your eyes and take a minivacation (picture yourself in your favorite place, perhaps soaking up the sun on a Caribbean beach).

Be sure to give yourself lots of positive affirmations. Write your affirmations down and post them on your phone and around your desk. And read them, often!

AFFIRMATIONS

- **I am offering customers something of value!**
- **I am terrific at my job!**
- **When customers say no, they are not rejecting me!**

CHAPTER 21

"I'M SO*OOO* MAD!"

It's hard to know what to do with a customer's anger when it hits you. The first impulse is to duck—"Don't yell at me, *I* didn't do it!"—or to lob a little fire and brimstone right back at the customer. Neither option is good for business, or good for you.

Some callers are angry before they call you, others become angry during the call—often unexpectedly. In either situation, the angry caller is likely to throw you off pace. After all, when you're dealing over the telephone lines, you seldom get to see the anger coming.

When customer anger goes unresolved, you can't learn anything from that transaction, so you can't learn what went wrong or how to correct it. It's worth your effort to turn an irate customer around. Think of it this way: The word *irate* "turned around" is *etari,* and the letters is *etari* could stand for "in *Every Tantrum* is *A Real Insight."* If you don't espouse this idea and work to turn your customer around, he or she may well be lost forever. And without customers, there's really not much reason for you to be staffing that phone.

Dealing positively with customer anger is positive for you. When you duck customer anger, or respond in kind, you say to yourself that you are powerless—that you can't do anything to improve the situation. That message will wear down your self-esteem faster than just about anything.

Managing customer anger in a positive way requires that you learn to think about anger in a new way. When customers express anger to you, it is a sign that they care what happens, that they want a positive solution. That's a gift that customers bring to you. With that gift, you have the opportunity to make something good happen, and to keep the customer. Do what your Mom and Dad taught you to do whenever you got a gift—including the ones you didn't like. *Thank* customers for bringing their anger to you. If you don't, you can bet they'll be sharing it with their friends— and with your other customers.

After you acknowledge a customer's anger and allow the customer to vent, you are ready to move into real problem solving. The six-step Service Recovery model developed by Ron Zemke and Chip Bell works well. While not all customers require you to use all six steps, it's a good rule of thumb that the angrier your customer is, the further down the recovery road you will have to travel.

THE ROAD TO SERVICE RECOVERY

1. *Apologize.* **Acknowledge your customer's feelings and apologize for the inconvenience.**
2. *Listen, empathize, and ask open questions.* **Use your skills to show your customer that you care and want to learn about the problem.**
3. *Fix the problem quickly and fairly.* **Do whatever is required to give your customer the product or service originally expected.**
4. *Offer atonement.* **Sometimes doing what was supposed to be done in the first place isn't enough. A gesture of atonement says, "I want to make it up to you."**
5. *Keep your promises.* **Service breakdowns begin when your customer believes your service promise has been broken. Be certain that you keep the promises you make, and make only promises you can keep, during the recovery process.**
6. *Follow up.* **After you implement your solution,**

follow up in your company. Did the new order ship as promised? Was the original problem fixed? Also, follow up with your customer. Did the solution work? Is your customer satisfied?

WHEN CUSTOMER ANGER BLOCKS PROBLEM SOLVING

Sometimes a customer's anger, or the way it is expressed, can prevent you from effective problem solving. While it is easy to say, "It's okay. In this customer's mind, I am the company. The customer is mad at the company, not at me personally," it can feel very, very personal.

It is perfectly all right to stop and ask your customer, "Have I done something personally to upset you? Because if I have, I'd really like to correct it. I would really like to be on your side in helping get to a solution." This statement has the same effect on many customers as transferring the call to a supervisor. It gives the customer cause to pause and takes some of the offensive out of his or her telephone talk.

A FEW WORDS ABOUT FOUL LANGUAGE

Some customers have the unfortunate proclivity toward foul language; the angrier they are, the bluer their language becomes. If you aren't bothered or upset by it, great. If you are, you have a right not to listen to it.

Check your company's policy regarding foul language from customers before you take any action. Your boss may want you to transfer all such calls to him or her, or to another supervisor (and, of course, when the transfer is complete the swear words will stop). If you are asked to handle foul language on your own, a technique that works well is to say something like:

"I'm very sorry. I want to help, but I find foul language
upsetting. Can we try again?"

or

"I would really like to help you, but I will have to hang
up if I continue to hear foul language."

If you tell the caller you will hang up if the swearing doesn't
stop, and the word choices don't change during the next
three or four sentences, hang up! You build "contractual
trust" when you do this: You made a promise of action and
you followed through on it. Forty-nine customers out of
fifty will call back, and *apologize to you*. The fiftieth will call
your manager. That's okay, because you will have talked to
your manager and he or she will be ready and waiting for
the call.

The key to effectively handling angry customers lies in not
becoming caught up in their emotions. When you stay
professional, you are in a position to help—even if the only
help they need is for someone to listen.

CHAPTER 22

ENDING THE ENDLESS CALL

You know who they are. They call on your busiest day, when you've got eight calls to return, an important project to complete, and the need to walk out the front door at 5:00 P.M. sharp. They're the callers who don't want to end the call. They want to tell you about their lives, their coworkers, their families in minute detail, and to recount the story of their last hospital visit in real time.

Worse—they're your customers. And you don't know how to get them off the phone without being rude!

Relax. These customers, and their phone calls, can be managed. One of the following simple techniques should do the trick:

• *Set out the ground rules.* If you are calling or are taking a call from a known talker, you aren't being offensive when you take the offensive. Before the conversation begins, set the time parameter. Do it in a way that makes your customer feel important—"Mr. Whitmore, I'm glad I reached you. I'm pushed for time, but I wanted to return my most important calls. Do you have ten minutes so we can discuss the product shipping information you requested? Or is there a better time for me to call?" A statement like this flatters your customer by suggesting that he is a busy and important person. It allows you to work the conversation to a close with a statement like, "Wow, we really got a lot accomplished. But I promised this would only take ten minutes, and we're at that now. Thank you so much for taking the time now to talk with me."

• *Don't play the waiting game.* Some people are just born talkers. They don't even mind if you're not really listening so long as they're not talking to themselves. So they talk and talk and talk and talk, and you "uh huh" and "oh" and "I see" and hope that eventually they'll run down and let you off the phone. They won't. This is a waiting game that you will lose every time.

So why do you keep playing? Most likely you fear that they will take offense if you try to end the conversation. They won't—if you do it in a courteous and direct manner. (They may even be secretly thankful for the help—some people just don't know how to end a conversation.) You may have to jump in when they pause for breath, but don't beat around the bush or drop hints. Just say it—"Gee, Terry, it's been great talking with you, but I have to sign off for now."

If your conversation calls for action on your part, you can include that—"Terry, I'm so glad you called. I'm going to let you go so I can look up those files right now and find the information you need. Okay?" What can Terry say but "Okay"? And when Terry does, it's time for you to say goodbye.

• *Listen some more.* When setting ground rules and being direct doesn't work, listen some more. Your customer may be trying to tell you something important that you're not hearing. If the phone conversation is about a product or service problem, it may be that your customer is still venting. Some people need to let off a lot of steam when things go wrong. While that isn't always pleasant to hear, and doesn't always seem to be helpful in resolving the problem, remember that angry customers need to vent. If you abruptly end the conversation, the customer is apt to vent to friends and family—and to your other customers and potential customers.

It may also be that the customer doesn't believe that you've understood the message he or she is trying to convey. Perhaps the customer is doing a poor job of explaining, or perhaps you've jumped to the wrong conclusion—and offered the wrong solution. Use your listening skills and the

technique of reflective listening—repeating what the customer has said in a summarized form—to increase and
confirm your understanding.

• *Use "I" statements and a promise of action.* What if the
customer keeps talking, you've tried the techniques, they
aren't working, and you *still need* to end the conversation? It
helps to include a statement of action, including when and
how the customer will know you've taken that action:

Wrong: "*You* need to let me get off the phone, Ms. Wallace,
              if *you* expect me to do anything about this."

Right: "*I* appreciate your concern, Ms. Wallace. *I* need to
              take some time to review the information you've
              given me so that *I* can take action to correct the
              immediate problem with your account. You'll see
              the correction on your next statement."

PART

III

MANAGING
YOURSELF

The most important person to manage in any telephone conversation is *you*. Fortunately, of all the things you manage, the thing you have the most control over is yourself. All you need to do is choose to exercise it.

If you don't manage yourself—if you are unaware of your own voice, or you are too tired or too stressed to care—chances are slim that any call you handle will leave a positive memory with your customer or a positive "job well done" feeling with you.

Managing yourself means understanding and paying attention to the communication qualities and tone of your voice—and making a commitment to continually build on your vocal skills. It means learning how to ease the emotional labor of telephone talk by managing your own telephone stress level.

CHAPTER 23

YOUR PHONE VOICE

Few people are aware of how much the telephone changes vocal quality. Even with fiber optic cable, telephones distort the tones and shadings that give your voice "personality." In fact, speech consultant Ralph Proodian contends that a Caruso vintage 78 rpm record provides better tonal quality than a standard telephone!

Telephone distortion may create a simple annoyance—such as giving your voice a nasal tone—or it may totally change the meaning of your message—by making you sound threatening when you mean to sound committed, or condescending when you mean to sound concerned. It isn't hard to understand, then, why becoming aware of and working to improve your telephone voice is so important. In this chapter, we'll examine your voice and how the telephone changes it. Chapter 24 offers specific tips for your own personal voice improvement program.

SEE YOUR VOICE

Sound impossible? It's not. Close your eyes and listen to your own voice during a business call, or listen while talking to a friend or family member. Picture the person who belongs to that voice. Is the person friendly or furious? Helpful or harassing? This is the picture your caller may have every time he or she talks with you.

Your voice is created by a combination of your breath control (this gives your voice its power), tone (created as the air moves from your lungs through your larynx), and your pronunciation (how you form particular sounds with your "articulators," e.g., mouth, teeth, lips, and lower jaw).

BREATH CONTROL

Proper breath control is a function of proper posture, good health, and good habits. Your lungs and diaphragm can't work effectively if you are slumped at your desk, so make a habit of sitting up straight when you talk on the telephone. And the better your physical condition, the better your lung capacity. On the telephone, that translates into being able to speak without the soft, breathy quality that may be misunderstood.

TONE

Your emotional state will modify your pitch range, whether you intend it to or not. When you are stressed or angry or excited or surprised or, whatever, it *will* come through in your voice. And you can bet that your customer will pay more attention to this subverbal message than to the actual words that you use. You can manage this effect through concentration and practice, but you cannot eliminate it.

PRONUNCIATION

The way you use your articulators will not only form the words you use but also your own individual speech patterns. The pronunciation and intonation patterns you use are learned and reflect the region of the country where you grew up, your social group, and perhaps even your ethnic heritage.

It's impossible to speak clearly when you're chewing gum or eating or have a cigarette in your mouth.

There are no intrinsically right or wrong speech patterns. However, be aware of your own accent and vocal patterns and consider whether or not they serve you well at work. A regional accent may make you more accepted with a particular areas of the country, but as the telephone lines bring you closer to distant customers, does that same accent interfere with clear communication? A good friend from Northern Minnesota once had to "hand off" a customer call—the customer, from Georgia, couldn't understand a word she said.

Your telephone voice reveals your personality. It is the number one way that the customer on the other end of the line gets to know you as an individual. Five qualities combine to make your telephone voice your own.

Five Qualities of a Good Telephone Voice

1. *Alertness.* Your voice should have spark and energy. Give the customer the impression that you are wide-awake and alert—and anxious to help.
2. *Pleasantness.* Your voice should be smooth, not jarring or whiney. Communicate with your voice that you are a pleasant and happy person. There is no room for shortness or anger.
3. *Conversational tone.* You are a real human being talking with (not at) another real human being. Even when using a script or job aid, work hard to keep your tone conversational and your language simple and straightforward.
4. *Distinctness.* Use clear articulation and enunciation. All of us tend to get lazy in our face-to-face speech—we drop the final consonant or breeze through that middle syllable. The telephone exaggerates this tendency, so open your mouth and let the sound come out clearly.
5. *Expressiveness.* Vary your tone and rate. Build a verbal picture with your voice.

CHAPTER 24

A PLAN FOR VOICE IMPROVEMENT

The following improvement plan has two focuses. The first is to improve your general vocal quality. The second is to improve your communication effectiveness, that is, your ability to communicate courtesy and helpfulness—the two basic customer expectations. Naturally, these two elements are intertwined: Improved vocal quality will help you communicate better, and good word choice and listening skills won't mean a thing if the caller can't understand you.

VOCAL QUALITY

To begin, conduct your own vocal assessment. Using your everyday telephone voice, tape record yourself reading this Vocal Quality Test Paragraph:

VOCAL QUALITY TEST PARAGRAPH

Providing great service over the telephone is a tough job. I know the telephone has an impact on how I communicate my message. But even without nonverbal communication, I can still use the telephone as a powerful tool for communicating with my customers. To do this, I carefully craft my message— paying close attention to the words and explanations I will use. I work hard to let my personality show through my voice quality, and to keep my tone upbeat and my pronunciation clear. Sometimes I wonder how my voice actually sounds to my customers. Do I sound bored? Aggressive? Sincere? Friendly? To find out, I listen to myself and I ask friends and coworkers to critique my telephone voice. When my voice sounds tired, they let me know. That helps me put the spark back. And when I'm doing great—well, it's nice to have someone tell me so.

Time how long you took to read the paragraph, and assess your vocal quality using the Vocal Qualities Checklist below (photocopy the checklist so you can use it again). If you have the time (and the courage), invite a friend or coworker to listen and evaluate with you.

VOCAL QUALITIES CHECKLIST

Check the appropriate boxes in order to identify your strengths and areas for improvement.

Rate:

Slow (over 80 seconds) ☐

Good (1 minute) ☐

Fast (under 50 seconds) ☐

Volume:

Too soft ☐

Just right ☐

Too loud ☐

Clarity:

Overenunciated, sounded mechanical ☐

Enunciated well, each word was clear ☐

Mumbled, slurred words or dropped endings ☐

Pitch:

Too high, sounded whiney ☐

Too low, sounded gravelly ☐

Monotonous, no variation ☐

Good, sounded natural and varied ☐

Tone:

Friendly ☐

Sincere ☐

Overly enthusiastic ☐

Pushy ☐

Timid ☐

Confident ☐

Maintain and date your evaluation and make a note on your calendar to reevaluate your voice in three weeks, to see how you've progressed. If you don't want to use the test paragraph, any paragraph 150 words in length will do.

Much improvement can be made by simply being aware of what you need to change. If you speak too fast or too slow, or too loud or too softly, enlist several friends and coworkers into your improvement effort. Ask them to tell you—or signal you—when you are "doing it again." Notice *when* it happens. You may speak too fast when you are excited, or become too soft when faced with an angry caller.

If your tone is off kilter, ask youself why. Are you timid because you fear giving wrong information: Are you overly enthusiastic because you think you need more "personality" to do telephone sales? When you are comfortable with your role on the phone, it will be reflected in your vocal tone.

COMMUNICATION EFFECTIVENESS

Improving the effectiveness of each telephone call is just as important as improving your telephone voice. Ask a manager or coworker to listen to you while you talk on the telephone to customers, or set a recorder by your phone and tape about fifteen minutes worth of calls. Using the Telephone Effectiveness Checklist on the next page (again, you'll want to photocopy it), rate your performance. The "best" rating for each question may vary with your company standards and policies, and not every question will be relevant to the types of calls you are making. When that's the case, just skip the question and move on.

TELEPHONE EFFECTIVENESS CHECKLIST

Promptness of answer: _____ Rings

	Yes	**No**
Greeting:		
Did you use a salutation?	☐	☐
Did you use a clear and appropriate identification statement?	☐	☐
Did you ask how you could help?	☐	☐
Did your tone establish rapport?	☐	☐
Was the call transferred to you?	☐	☐
If "yes," how many times was the caller transferred?	_____ Times	
Were you able to help the caller during this call?	☐	☐
Did you transfer the call?	☐	☐
If "yes," did you preview the transfer process?	☐	☐
Did you offer the name and number that you were transferring to?	☐	☐
Did you "walk" the caller through the transfer (staying on the line until it was successfully completed)?	☐	☐
Did you place the caller on hold?	☐	☐
Was hold appropriate?	☐	☐
Did you ask the customer's permission?	☐	☐
Did you check back regularly (every 30 seconds)?	☐	☐
Did you thank the customer for holding?	☐	☐
Did you take a message?	☐	☐
Did you gather complete information (i.e., the caller's name, company name, phone number, and other relevant data)?	☐	☐
Did you confirm the spelling and the phone number with the caller?	☐	☐
Were you able to answer the caller's questions or quickly refer the caller to the proper person or department?	☐	☐
Did you make the customer feel that you knew what you are doing and that he or she had called the right place?	☐	☐
Were you courteous and respectful?	☐	☐

CHAPTER 25

MENDING FRAYED NERVES

Telephone talk, whether you spend eight hours or eight minutes on the phone, is stressful. With over half of your normal communication information (the nonverbals) missing, you need to concentrate doubly hard to understand and to make yourself understood.

In addition to the mental concentration, telephones can cause physical stress. Do a quick check in your own office. How many people do you see talking on the telephone slumped down in their chairs, cradling the handset between their chins and shoulders, while they try to type or shuffle papers? Probably too many.

MANAGING PHYSICAL STRESS

If you spend a lot of time on the telephone, consider trading in your handset for a headset. They aren't expensive, they plug into your existing phone equipment, and they can cure a pain in the neck. They also keep the mouthpiece in position so your voice doesn't fade out as you move. (If you use a speaker phone to give you freedom of movement, consider whether or not a headset with a long cord might serve you equally well.)

There is no law that says that you have to sit to use the telephone. In fact, some salespeople report better results when they stand during calls. Why? It's easier for your voice to work when you are standing. And the act of standing, and maybe walking a few steps, can give you energy that is transferred to your phone voice.

Be sure to pause during busy phone days to stretch your muscles—especially those shoulder muscles. Try rolling your shoulders forward five times, and then backward five times. Then put your hands on your shoulders and massage those muscles at the base of your neck. Feels great, doesn't it!

MANAGING MENTAL STRESS

Even the most pleasant customers demand your full attention and concentration if the service encounter is to be successful. Try to take short stress-breaks. You can use this time to catch up on paperwork while you get away from the ringing phone. (Make sure, however, that you've arranged for someone else to take those customer calls.)

Sometimes the mental stress of telephone talk comes because we are uncomfortable making or receiving calls from customers. If that's the case for you, consider using Mental Visualization (see the chart on the next page). You'll find that visualizing phone calls in a positive and safe setting will take the fear and anxiety out of telephone talk.

MENTAL VISUALIZATION

First, make a telephone-calling comfort ladder. Visualize yourself making the following ten phone calls. As you do, rate the stress level you feel as a result of the imaginary call and write it to the right of the description (1 = no stress; 10 = extreme stress).

- Your spouse/significant other from your office to say hello _____
- Your boss _____
- Your mother- or father-in-law _____
- An established customer _____
- A repair shop to check on repair progress _____
- A prospective customer you've never met _____
- A respondent to a newspaper classified advertisement _____
- A friend from the office _____
- A potential customer whom a satisfied customer asked you to call _____
- Your banker _____
- A potential customer you met at a party _____
- A close relative _____

When you've rated each imaginary call, list the six *most* stressful calls on the stress ladder below (1 is most stressful, 2 is second most stressful, and so on).

1. _____
2. _____
3. _____
4. _____
5. _____
6. _____

Now, go one rung at a time. Write your sixth most stressful call on this line:

_____

(You will repeat this process for each of the calls on your stress ladder, working up to your most stressful call.)
Now, identify a person and a phone number that fits this situation:

_____   _____

(name)   (number)

Follow this routine:

1. Breathe deeply.
2. Visualize making the call:
   —See yourself seated at the phone.
   —See yourself looking up the number.
   —See yourself writing down the things you want to accomplish in the call.
   —See yourself dialing.
   —See yourself saying "hello" and identifying yourself by name.
   —See yourself making small talk.
   —See yourself saying, "Besides saying hello, the reason I called is to [one of your two objectives]."
   —See yourself relaxed and enjoying the call.
   —See yourself hanging up the phone.
3. Estimate your stress level (write it down).
4. Reward yourself.

Alternate between visualization and real practice. If, during a visualization you feel your stress level rising, immediately stop, take several deep breaths, and stop your negative thoughts. When you are back in control, return to visualizing the scene.

Adapted from *Stressless Selling*, revised edition, by Frances Meritt Stern and Ron Zemke, AMACOM Books, New York, 1990.

CHAPTER 26

"DO YOU MIND? IT'S PERSONAL!"

Some employers solve the dilemma of personal calls at work with a simple directive—they aren't allowed. If your employer has a "no personal calls" policy, your best bet is to respect it. Chances are that the policy is there for a good reason—after all, business phones need to be available for business customers.

Unfortunately, most of the people you do personal business with—bankers and doctors, for example—work the same hours you do. If you do need to make a personal call or if you need to receive a call due to a special or emergency situation, talk with your supervisor. Chances are, he or she will find a way to accommodate you.

When personal calls are a part of your business day, it's a good idea to keep some simple guidelines in mind:

1. Have a good reason for making or taking a personal call. Checking in on a sick child is a good reason; talking about the movies you've seen this week is not.
2. Keep personal calls short. When you're at work and not on break, your time isn't your own.
3. Don't take or make personal calls during peak business hours unless the situation is an emergency.
4. Don't use your employer's long distance account to place long distance personal calls. There is a misperception that once a business pays for a WATS-type service, it doesn't matter how many long distance calls are placed. That is no longer the case. Businesses

pay for the amount of time employees are on long distance.

PRIVACY

Personal privacy can be an issue when you take personal calls at work. If you are uncomfortable discussing your latest physical exam or the state of your finances within the hearing of your coworkers, ask if you can return the call in the evening. More and more businesses offer extended hours of telephone service for their customers, and they may be happy to talk with you after 5:00 P.M. if you request it.

If you must take or make a personal call, and don't have your own office with a door, consider asking someone who does to lend you his or her office. Be prepared to offer some explanation of the situation, and be sure to keep the conversation as short as possible.

HARASSMENT

U.S. federal and state laws offer protection from harassing and annoying telephone calls. Among the types of phone calls that may be considered in violation of these laws are threats of violence or damage to your reputation (including "if you don't . . . , I'm going to tell your boss"), causing your telephone to ring continuously, repeatedly calling with an intent to annoy, or calling at your place of employment after being informed that your employer prohibits such calls.

If you are receiving telephone calls that you believe are harassing or abusive, call your local telephone company, attorney, or police department to learn about your rights and to put an end to the calls.

APPENDIX A

PLACING AN INTERNATIONAL CALL

If your company does business with customers outside of the United States, identify and keep a list of the individuals in your company who speak other languages. Their skills may be invaluable as you communicate with customers in or from a foreign country.

To place most international station-to-station calls, dial the following:

- The international access code (011)
- The country code
- The city code
- The local phone number

Allow at least 45 seconds after dialing your international call for ringing to begin.

Below is a list of country and city (routing) codes. Contact your long distance company if you have difficulty placing a long distance call.

Algeria 213★
American Samoa 386★
Argentina 54
Buenos Aires 1
Cardoba 51
Aruba 297
All points 8
Australia 61

The following Caribbean countries may be reached by dialing 1 + 809 + local number: Angu lla, Antigua (and Barbuda), Bahamas, Barbados, Bermuda, British Virgin Islands, Cayman Islands, Dominica, Dominican Republic, Grenada (and Carriacou), Jamaica, Montserrat, Nevis, St. Kitts, St. Lucia, St. Vincent and the Grenadines, Trinidad and Tobago, and Turks and Caicos Islands.
★City code not required.
★★Call your long distance company for special instructions.

Canberra 62
Melbourne 3
Sydney 2
Austria 43
Graz 316
Innsbruck 5222
Vienna 1 or 222
Bahrain 973★
Bangladesh 880
Dhaka 2
Belgium 32
Antwerp 3
Brussels 2
Belize 501
Belize City 2
Bolivia 591
La Paz 2
Brazil 55
Brasillia 61
Rio de Janeiro 21
Sao Paulo 11
Bulgaria 359
Sofia 2
Chile 56
Santiago 2
China 86
Beijiing 1
Shanghai 21
Columbia 57
Bogota 1
Cartagena 59
Costa Rica 506★
Cyprus 357
Nicosia 2
Czechoslovakia 42
Brno 5
Prague 2
Denmark 45
Copenhagen 3
(suburbs 4)
Ecuador 593
Quito 2
Egypt 20
Alexandria 3
Cairo 2

El Salvador 503★
Ethiopia 251
Addis Ababa 1
Fiji Islands 679★
Finland 358
Helsinki 0
France 33
Lyon 7
Marseille 91
Paris 1
French Polynesia (Tahiti) 689★
Germany (former FRG) 49
Berlin 30
Bonn 228
Frankfurt 69
Hamburg 40
Munich 89
Germany (former GDR) 37
Berlin 2
Dresden 51
Leipzig 41
Greece 30
Athens 1
Salonica 31
Guam 671★
Guatemala 502
Guatemala City 2
All others 9
Guyana 592
Georgetown 2
Haiti 509
Port au Prince 1
Honduras 504★
Hong Kong 852
Kowloon 3
Hungary 36
Budapest 1
Iceland 354
Keflavik 2
Reykjavik 1
India 82
Calcutta 33
New Delhi 11
Indonesia 62

Jakarta 21
Iran 98
Teheran 21
Iraq 964
Baghdad 1
Ireland 353
Dublin 1
Cork 21
Israel 972
Haifa 4
Jerusalem 2
Tel Aviv 3
Italy 39
Milan 2
Naples 81
Rome 6
Venice 41
Ivory Coast 225★
Japan 81
Hiroshima 81
Kobe 78
Osaka 6
Tokyo 3
Yokohama 45
Jordan 962
Amman 6
Kenya 254
Mambasa 11
Nairobi 2
Korea 82
Pusan 51
Seoul 2
Kuwait 965★
Liberia 231★
Libya 218
Behghazi 61
Tripoli 21
Liechtenstein 41
All points 75
Luxembourg 352★
Malaysia 60
Kualo Lumpir 3
Maldives 960★
Malta 356★
Mauritius 230★

Mexico★★
Monaco 33
All points 93
Morocco 212
Casablanca★
Robat 7
Netherlands 31
Amsterdam 20
Rotterdam 10
The Hague 70
Netherlands Antilles 51
Bonaire 7
Curacao 9
St. Maarten 5
New Zealand 64
Auckland 9
Wellington 4
Nicaragua 505
Managua 2
Nigeria 234
Lagos 1
Norway 47
Bergen 5
Oslo 2
Pakistan 92
Islamabad 51
Karachi 21
Panama 507★
Paraguay 595
Asuncion 21
Peru 51
Lima 14
Philippines 63
Cebu City 32
Manila 2
Subic Bay 47
Poland 48
Crakow 12
Warsaw 22
Portugal 351
Lisbon 1
Qatar 974★
Romania 49
Bucharest 0
Saudi Arabia 966

Dhahran 3
Jeddah 2
Makkah (Mecca) 2
Riyadh 1
Senegal 221★
Singapore 65★
South Africa 27
Cape Town 21
Johannesburg 11
Pretoria 12
Spain 34
Barcelona 3
Las Palmas (Canary Islands) 28
Madrid 1
Sri Lanka 94
Colombo 1
Suriname 597★
Sweden 46
Goteborg 31
Stockholm 8
Switzerland 41
Berne 31
Geneva 22
Zurich 1
Taiwan 886
Taipei 2
Tanzania 255
Dar es Salaam 51
Thailand 66
Bangkok 2
Tunisia 216
Tunis 1
Turkey 90
Ankara 1

Istanbul 1
Uganda 256
Kampala 41
USSR 7
Moscow 095
United Arab Emirates 971
Abu Dhabi 2
Dubai 4
United Kingdom 44
Belfast 232
Cardiff (Wales) 222
Edinburgh (Scotland) 41
Liverpool 51
London
    Inner city 71
    Other areas 81
Uruguay 598
Montevideo 2
Vatican City 39
All points 6
Venezuela 58
Caracas 2
Maracaibo 61
Yemen 967
Sanaa 2
Yugoslavia 38
Belgrade 11
Zagreb 51
Zaire 243
Kinshasa 12
Zambia 260
Lusaka 1
Zimbabwe 263
Harare 4

APPENDIX B

NORTH AMERICAN AREA CODES

Area Code	Location	Area Code	Location
*201	New Jersey	*315	New York
202	District of Columbia	*316	Kansas
203	Connecticut	*317	Indiana
204	Manitoba	318	Louisiana
205	Alabama	*319	Iowa
*206	Washington	*401	Rhode Island
207	Maine	*402	Nebraska
208	Idaho	403	Alberta, Yukon,
*209	California		Northwest
*212	New York		Territories
*213	California	*404	Georgia
*214	Texas	405	Oklahoma
*215	Pennsylvania	*406	Montana
*216	Ohio	*407	Florida
*217	Illinois	*408	California
*218	Minnesota	*409	Texas
*219	Indiana	*410	Maryland
*301	Maryland	*412	Pennsylvania
302	Delaware	*413	Massachusetts
*303	Colorado	*414	Wisconsin
304	West Virginia	*415	California
*305	Florida	*416	Ontario
306	Saskatchewan	*417	Missouri
307	Wyoming	*418	Quebec
*308	Nebraska	419	Ohio
*309	Illinois	*501	Arkansas
*310	California	502	Kentucky
*312	Illinois	*503	Oregon
*313	Michigan	504	Louisiana
*314	Missouri	505	New Mexico

States or provinces that are serviced by more than one area code are shown by asterisk (*).

93

Area Code	Location	Area Code	Location
*506	New Brunswick	*712	Iowa
*507	Minnesota	*713	Texas
*508	Massachusetts	*714	California
*509	Washington	*715	Wisconsin
*510	California	*716	New York
*512	Texas	*717	Pennsylvania
*513	Ohio	*718	New York
*514	Quebec	*719	Colorado
*515	Iowa	801	Utah
*516	New York	802	Vermont
*517	Michigan	803	South Carolina
*518	New York	*804	Virginia
519	Ontario	*805	California
601	Mississippi	*806	Texas
602	Arizona	*807	Ontario
603	New Hampshire	808	Hawaii
604	British Columbia	809	Puerto Rico
605	South Dakota	*812	Indiana
*606	Kentucky	*813	Florida
*607	New York	*814	Pennsylvania
*608	Wisconsin	*815	Illinois
*609	New Jersey	*816	Missouri
*612	Minnesota	*817	Texas
*613	Ontario	*818	California
*614	Ohio	*819	Quebec
*615	Tennessee	*901	Tennessee
*616	Michigan	902	Prince Edward Island and Nova Scotia
*617	Massachusetts	*903	Texas
*618	Illinois	*904	Florida
*619	California	*906	Michigan
701	North Dakota	907	Alaska
702	Nevada	*908	New Jersey
*703	Virginia	*912	Georgia
*704	North Carolina	*913	Kansas
*705	Ontario	*914	New York
*707	California	*915	Texas
*708	Illinois	*916	California
709	Newfoundland/ Labrador	*918	Oklahoma
		*919	North Carolina

APPENDIX C

TIME ZONE MAP

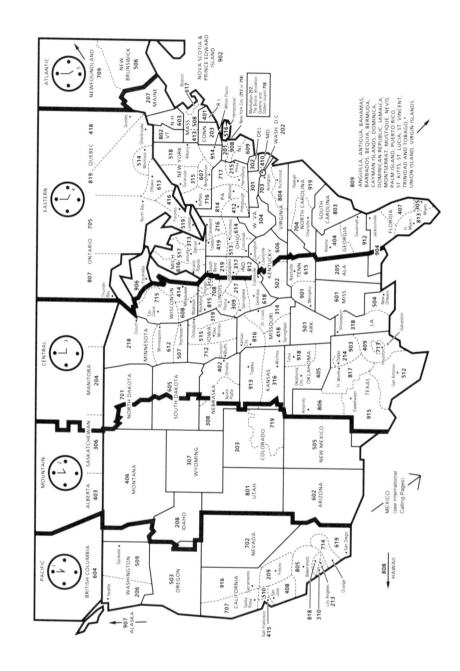

APPENDIX D

VERBAL SPELLING GUIDE

Perhaps you've heard the old story about the woman who moved from Iowa to a small town in Connecticut. Anxious to fit in with the locals, she listened for colloquial phrases. One day she overheard two farmers discussing high prices. "It cost me a nominal egg," the first farmer complained. For months, she used this phrase when talking to friends and family members, never quite sure just what "a nominal egg" was. Finally, the cashier at the local checkout counter asked her what she meant.

"Why, isn't that something you people say around here?"

"No," replied the cashier with a puzzled look. Then her face broke out into a smile. "Not," she said, speaking slowly and carefully, "unless you mean, 'It cost me an arm and a leg.' "

Many consonants sound alike when you are talking on the phone, and the same consonant or vowel is often pronounced quite differently by people from different regional or ethnic backgrounds.

When such misunderstandings happen over the telephone, your customer may not be sure if you've said "Paul" or "Dahl" or "Ball." The easiest way to clarify the situation is by spelling out the word—"The last name is Dahl, 'D' as in 'David,' 'A' as in 'apple,' 'H' as in 'hunt,' 'L' as in 'love.' "

When you are on the spot, it can be difficult to think of spelling guide words, so below is a handy list for you to use. Notice that by each alphabet letter there are spaces for you to write your own preferred words. Consider using a word that is related to your business or to your customer. For example, "Yes, this is the EGS Paper Company. 'E' as in 'excellent,' 'G' as in 'great,' and 'S' as in 'savings.' "

A	Apple		I	Ice Cream

_____

_____

B	Best		J	Jack

_____

_____

C	Customer		K	Kite

_____

_____

D	Dance		L	Love

_____

_____

E	Eat		M	Money

_____

_____

F	Frank		N	Nancy

_____

_____

G	Grand		O	Open

_____

_____

H	Hat		P	Peter

Q   Quick   V   Victor

_____   _____

_____   _____

R   Rain   W   Washer

_____   _____

_____   _____

S   Super   X   X Ray

_____   _____

_____   _____

T   Truck   Y   Yes

_____   _____

_____   _____

U   Unicorn   Z   Zebra

_____   _____

_____   _____